Testing English

Also available from Continuum

Rethinking English in Schools, Viv Ellis, Carol Fox and Brian Street
Teaching Creativity, Derek Pigrum

Testing English

Formative and Summative Approaches to English Assessment

Bethan Marshall

continuum

Continuum International Publishing Group

The Tower Building　　　　80 Maiden Lane
11 York Road　　　　　　　Suite 704
London SE1 7NX　　　　　　New York, NY 10038

www.continuumbooks.com

British Library Cataloguing-in-Publication Data
A catalogue record for this book is available from the British Library.

ISBN:　978-1-4411-9426-8 (paperback)
　　　　978-1-4411-8293-7 (hardcover)

Library of Congress Cataloging-in-Publication Data
Marshall, Bethan, 1958–
Testing English : formative and summative approaches to English assessment / Bethan Marshall.
　　p. cm.
Includes bibliographical references.
ISBN: 978-1-4411-8293-7 (pbk.)
1. Language arts–Ability testing. 2. Educational tests and measurements–Evaluation. I. Title.
LB1576.M3789 2010
428.0076–dc22　　　　　　　　　　　　　　　2010020336

Typeset by Newgen Imaging Systems Pvt Ltd, Chennai, India
Printed and bound in India by Replika Press Pvt Ltd

Dedicated to
Myfanwy and Angharad

Contents

REF *

Acknowledgements

This book would not have been possible were it not for the countless teachers who gave up their time to be involved in the various projects on which I write. So I want to thank first all those teachers who took part in KMOFAP, KOSAP and LHTL. In particular, I want to thank one teacher, Ellie Bongers, who was killed just after Christmas, 2009. I would also like to thank the four researchers who helped in the projects Clare Lee, Dave Pedder, Joanna Swann and Nicola Serret without whose help the interviews would never have been completed. I would like to thank also those involved in the various research teams I have worked on at Kings, including Paul Black, Christine Harrison, Jeremy Hodgen and Dylan Wiliam, whose ideas have been endlessly helpful. I would like to pay special tribute also to the LHTL team, in particular Mary James and John MacBeath, who have helped me develop and rethink much of what I originally thought, but also to Patrick Carmichael, Mary Jane Drummond, Alison Fox, Bob McCormick, Richard Proctor and Sue Swaffield.

Then there are the people who have had the painful experience of discussing various aspects of the book with me and even reading sections of it. I would like to thank Simon Gibbons for patiently listening to my thoughts on LATE and for his generous donations of some of the early documents written by James Britton. I would also like to thank again Jeremy Hodgen for his various comments on the KOSAP work and too Kate Spencer Ellis. I would like to thank Elizabeth Catherwood for her careful proof reading and Sue Brindley who was most helpful in all the advise and she gave while I was writing the book and for her remarks on the finished manuscript.

Finally I would like to thank my family, Richard, who encouraged me all the way, and my to daughters – Myfanwy and Angharad. It is to them that I owe the biggest debt because it is through them that I have witnessed all the struggles of the current exam system from KS1 through to A-level. In Chapter 2 official acknowledgement is given to the JMB for allowing access to confidential material. The JMB does not necessarily accept the views expressed in this chapter.

English and the Art of Language

Chapter Outline

This is a book about assessment, in particular assessment in English. English, as a subject, has had a curious relationship with those who want to see how pupils are doing in it, and it is nearly always one of complaint. Something about the system makes them wonder whether or not we are rewarding our pupils with the marks they deserve and so this is where we will begin. We will look at how English teachers have negotiated the summative assessment of their charges, considering first how they meandered through the strictures of exam board control after the Second World War and then were frogmarched through reforms, after the 1988 Education Reform Act to the present day, sometimes kicking, always screaming. Next we will look at how they have sought to reclaim the assessment agenda, this time not through summative assessment but via the formative kind, assessment for learning or AfL. Finally we will glance at another summative project before alighting on the assessment of English elsewhere in the world. And when all that is done we will conclude.

But the question we must ask first is why English teachers are so quarrelsome when it comes to assessing their subject. The answer that this book gives is that it is because in some shape or form they wish to see the subject assessed as an arts subject and that means concentrating more on the whole of what is written or said than its parts. Pat Creber, in a book entitled *Thinking through English*, describes the subject as 'untidy' (1990). His use of the word 'untidy' is interesting, for as far as I can tell he does not use the word critically, rather, I think, he thinks of English as one would a messy but endearing child, full of play but not very good at tidying up afterwards. In the play many exciting, unthought of adventures are embarked upon, many ordinary objects are sequestered for extraordinary use; the imagination is untamed. The problem is the mess that is left afterwards, and depending on one's view of English, this is either unproblematic, a bit tricky, or a vastly difficult dilemma needing a quick resolution. English, Creber is saying, does not colour between the lines but there are those who think it should.

In many ways this has always been the problem with English. There are those who think it should be a technical skill where the basics rules of reading and writing are taught through a combination of phonics and grammar. There are some who think it is essentially a form of communication where students are encouraged to write in clear concise prose. But there are those who think of English, certainly as including an ability to communicate, but more than that, they see the use of language as an art form. These individuals see words like an artist's brush strokes, a sentence like a musical phrase. They see a writer as someone who paints a picture in words and a reader as someone who has imagined themselves into a world of print. This is how this book sees English. It, too, sees language as an art and significantly this affects how English is assessed. In some ways it is easy to test the technical skills of a pupil, much harder to examine how creative they are or to form a sense of how they are progressing imaginatively.

A brief history of English as an art

Against the mechanical

Perhaps the most famous rendition of the world of the imagination clashing with the world of facts and hard edges is Dickens *Hard Times*, written in 1854, in which he explored the harsh utilitarian world of the northern industrialists with the kinder, more humane world of Sissy, a girl from Sleary's circus. Although the book, somewhat unsympathetically, looks at the rise of the trade unions, albeit in the world of the dark satanic mills, it has become famous for the schooling offered by one of the central characters – Gradgrind. Gradgrind inhabits an existence entirely dominated by facts. Nothing else matters and all is seen through this very tainted window. He runs his school through facts, even his life through facts,

> Thomas Gradgrind, sir. A man of realities. A man of facts and calculations . . . With a rule and a pair of scales, and the multiplication table always in his pocket, sir, ready to weigh and measure any parcel of human nature, and tell you exactly what it comes to. It is a mere question of figures, of simple arithmetic. (ibid., p. 10)

His children are 'never to wonder' at any point, only to deal with 'facts, facts, facts'. They have never listened to nursery rhymes, never seen a cow jumping over the moon but only dealt with the astronomical principles. Into this world of 'realities' comes Sissy who does not conform. Her world has sympathy, empathy and imagination which comes in part from Sleary, who at the end of the novel confesses, 'They can't be alwayth a learning, nor yet can they be alwayth a workin, they ain't made for it' (ibid., p. 282).

Dickens presents harsh reason against a world of fancy, the utilitarian against the irrepressible human spirit. Even Coketown, 'A town so sacred in fact, and so triumphant in its assertion of course got on well? Why no, not quite well. No? Dear me' (ibid., p. 28) doesn't thrive. And, with perhaps the greatest irony of all, at night it takes on a magical quality; the mills become 'Fairy palaces'.

In writing *Hard Times* Dickens was echoing in particular Thomas Carlyle, to whom he dedicated the book. Carlyle, in his essay 'Signs of the Times' (1829), wrote that he felt he was now living in a Mechanical Age, an Age of Machinery. And, he thought, this mechanization was likely to bring about, 'a mighty change in our whole manner of existence' (ibid., p. 67). The image of hard materialism, the mechanical, as opposed to the quintessentially softer and perhaps more wooly, floaty world of fancy has remained. Gradgrind's 'mere question of figures, of simple arithmetic' has dominated the education debate ever since. In a sense it has become almost pivotal in the discussion of the English curriculum. Is English an arts subject or a collection of facts, a set of rules, and, perhaps even more importantly, how can you assess it if it is the former?

Culture and the utilitarian

Writing shortly after Dickens' *Hard Times* Matthew Arnold observed, 'All test examinations . . . may be said to narrow reading upon a certain given point, and to make it mechanical' (Arnold, 1867, 1979, p. 95). The use of the phrase mechanical is telling in that it links him with Dickens and, more importantly, Carlyle, who as we have seen believed that culture and feeling were being strangled by utilitarianism; that which was artistic was being trampled in the dust by an age that was increasingly machine driven. In 1869 Arnold wrote *Culture and Anarchy*, in which again he reinforces the distinction between the artistic and the anarchic forces.

> Faith in machinery is, I said our besetting danger; often in machinery most absurdly disproportioned to the end which this machinery, if it is to do any good at all, is to serve; but always in machinery, as if it had a value in and for itself. (Arnold, 1869, 1948, p. 48)

Again we have references to the mechanical, and tellingly he writes that we have faith in it 'as if it had a value in and for itself'. Arnold, on the other hand, put his faith in the artistic. Having lost belief in God, as so many Victorians did, Arnold believed that the cultural and civilized things in life would be our salvation. Admittedly his beliefs were somewhat elitist. He did not question the class system in which he operated and the culture, which he so prized, could be threatened by the so-called masses. This could be explained by the French uprisings of 1848, but it can read uncomfortably today (Williams, 1961).

Nevertheless it is through his work as a schools' inspector that Arnold becomes more sympathetic, for here, as we have already seen, he rails against the exam system that they had in place at the time. In so doing he sounds like many English teachers today. The Revised Code, the framework under which Arnold operated as an HMI, came in to being in 1862 and had a very particular way of assessing children. In effect it brought about a system of payment by results. The school and particular teachers were paid by the success or otherwise of children passing an exam. Inspectors of schools, the earliest form of Her Majesty's Inspectors, went into schools and tested the children present. The visits were a kind of inspection and school's examination rolled into one.

It is apparent that Arnold felt constrained by the system and so continued in his criticisms of the testing regime. He went on to say that he felt inspections of schools were now governed by 'a narrowing system of test examinations' when there were 'organisations wanting to be guided by us into the best ways of learning and teaching' (Arnold, 1867, 1979, p. 95). He warned of the dangers of teaching to the test when the stakes were high, for the school grant depended on the pupils' success in the test.

> It tends to make instruction mechanical and to set a bar to duly extending it . . . [and] must inevitably concentrate the teachers' attention on producing this minimum and not simply on the good instruction of the school. The danger to be guarded against is the mistake of assuming these two – the producing of the minimum successfully and the good instruction of the school – as if they were identical. (ibid., p. 95)

In many ways, as has been suggested, his warnings are still pertinent today; the arguments about what is good for a person's education, the 'good instruction of the school', set against, for example, the position in the league tables, very relevant. He felt that the two were not necessarily the same. Two years earlier, he commented that,

> By ingenious preparation (as it is now found possible) to get children through the Revised Code examination in reading writing and ciphering, without their really knowing how to read write or cipher, so it will in practice, no doubt be found possible to get three fourths of the one fifth of the children over six through the examination in grammar, geography, and history, without their really knowing any one of these three matters. (ibid., p. 96)

In other words it was possible to pass the test without having gained any particular knowledge of the subject. For Arnold, 'More free play for the Inspector and more free play for the teacher is what is wanted' (ibid., p. 96). It is interesting that he wants 'free play'. Although he only mentions the inspector and teacher, one can only presume that he is referring to the children as well. While acknowledging, at another point, that much of the education children receive will of necessity be mechanical, he argues, 'But whatever introduces any sort of creative activity to relieve the passive reception of knowledge is valuable' (ibid., p. 97). He adds that subjects should be taught in a 'less mechanical and more interesting manner' so that they can 'call forth pleasurable activity' (ibid., p. 98).

Education, then, should be pleasurable, interesting and creative. In saying so Arnold sounds remarkably like the author David Almond, who, in his speech for being awarded the Carnegie Medal, had the temerity to attack the Labour Government's education policy of testing and target setting. The speech itself was reprinted in the Independent on the 15th July 1999. In it

Almond comments on a session that he taught in a primary school on *Skellig* and describes how at the end he encourages the pupils to write themselves: 'We play writing games that show just how vivid and how quick the imagination is for all of us' (Almond, 1999). He also tells of an imaginary teacher, who is an amalgamation of the good teachers he has seen in the past, called Mrs McKee. He argues that the Mrs Mckees of this world should, along with their charges, be allowed to escape the clutches of 'the world of assessment, accreditation, targets, scores, grades, tests and profiles . . . the bureaucratic nightmare' that 'entangles' (ibid.) her, for 10 per cent of the year. Almond concludes,

> There might be times when nothing is apparently going on, but we will accept your [Mrs McKee's] belief that there is a mysterious zone of the imagination, of intuition, of insight in which the beady gaze of the assessor and the record-keeper would be deadly. (ibid.)

Here again an author is contrasting what can be done in test conditions, the 'bureaucratic nightmare' under the all seeing eye of a clock and time-keeper with the more creative, 'mysterious zone' of the gifted teacher. In this 'zone' the pupils enter a world of 'imagination, of intuition, of insight'. In so doing he again marks out a landscape that is binary – the one of imagination versus the vulture like one of the 'beady' record-keeper: one where there are 'times where nothing is apparently going on' against 'assessment, accreditation, targets, scores, grades, tests and profiles'. Many of these are done by numbers – the targets, scores and tests – even grading turns letters into something numerically quantifiable. Only profiles are in any way descriptive.

Edmund Holmes, an HMI at the turn of the twentieth century also looks at the examination system. In his book, *What Is and What Might Be*, he criticizes what he sees as controlling force of exams on Western education. He asks:

> How did the belief that a formal examination is a worthy end for the teacher and child to aim at, and an adequate test of success in teaching and in learning, come to establish itself in this country? And not only in this country, but in the whole Western world? . . . In every Western country that is 'up to date' . . . the examination system controls education, and in doing so arrests the self-development of the child, and therefore strangles his inward growth. (Holmes, 1911, p. 8)

For Holmes the examination system is intimately connected with a view of the passive child he wishes to oppose.

Blind, passive, literal, unintelligent obedience is the basis on which the whole system of Western education has been reared . . . [The child] must become a tabula rasa before his teacher can begin to write on it. The vital part of him – call it what you will – must become clay before his teacher can begin to mould him. (ibid., p. 50)

It is the so-called 'moulding' of the child that he finds most offensive. A child should be allowed to grow without such interference but the exam system stops this. The teacher's,

business is to drill the child into the mechanical production of quasi-material results; and his success in doing this will be gauged in due course by an 'examination' – a periodic test which is designed to measure, not the degree of growth which the child has made, but the industry of the teacher as indicated by the receptivity of the class. (ibid., p. 51)

Again this echoes Almond's ponderings that for much of the time nothing in particular seems to be happening but actually the imagination is being fostered. So here, the 'drill' of 'the child into the mechanical production of quasi-material results' will stop the child from growth. Again Holmes' terminology keeps the image of Carlyle, with the word 'mechanical' but also reinforces the idea that the world of the imagination and growth lies separate from the world of numbers, of 'quasi-material results' and 'measure'.

What is also evident also from all three of these writers, separated by over a century, is that in so getting these results you are gaining nothing that really matters. The results are only 'quasi-material'; pupils may not 'really know[ing] any one of these . . . matters', it is all simply a 'bureaucratic nightmare' that tells us nothing. They are not part of a 'creative activity' or the 'mysterious zone of the imagination, of intuition, of insight'.

The difficulty with such a position is that it casts into doubt the whole purpose of assessment. There are some who might agree with this. Certainly the Newbolt Report of 1921 believed that it was impossible to assess a pupil's response to literature. For the writers of the report, English,

connotes the discovery of the world by the first and most direct way open to us, and the discovery of ourselves in our native environment . . . For the writing of English is essentially an art, and the effect of English literature, in education, is the effect of art upon the development of the human character. (Departmental Committee of the Board of Education [Newbolt Report], ch.1, para 14, p. 20)

Critical dissent

This then is one view of English as an art, both civilizing and somewhat mystical. There is, however, another: the idea of English, still as an arts subject but more one of critical dissent. Again it is worth looking at the origins of this view, which lie even earlier than Matthew Arnold and can be traced to the Dissenting schools and Academies. Originally the dissenters had dissented from The Act of Uniformity, passed by Parliament, in the mid-seventeenth century and this meant that they were effectively cut off from any mainstream education as this was either controlled by, or paid lip service to, the Church of England.

The Dissenting Academies, while religious in origin, were based on a precept that education was a source of social good. This came from a belief that people, while sinful, were rational. Learning to think and reason were integral to their view of the role of education as it extended these rational faculties. Reason, however, differed from the later Benthamite, or Utilitarian point of view, that we should reasonably do that which was beneficial to the greatest number of people, the view so parodied in *Hard Times*. The dissenters' particular take on the idea of the rational was that all are equal in the sight of God, the ultimately reasonable being, and which meant, in turn, that they believed in social equality and justice. This led, in turn, to support for the common man, a belief in his rights as a citizen and by association the English vernacular. Language was power.

In this respect the Dissenting Academies had much in common, as we shall see, with the later London School of English. The dissenters believed that English, not Latin (the chief subject in all public schools in England) should be the vehicle for both developing language and through language, independent thought. One of the chief exponents of such a move was William Enfield, a Presbyterian minister who taught at the Warrington Academy, where another radical thinker of the day, Joseph Priestley, also worked.

In 1774 William Enfield published what might loosely be conceived of as one of the first English text books for use in schools – *The Speaker: Or miscellaneous pieces selected from the best English writers, and disposed under the proper heads, with a view to facilitate the improvement of youth in reading and speaking*. Although the subheading tells you what to expect from the book as a whole the main title is *The Speaker*. In other words, in a book, the desired outcome is that the pupils should talk about, as well as read aloud, what they have read. They have to speak about it and, as the subheading suggests, they are discussing 'the best English writers'. Enfield did not confine his efforts to producing text books and was a regular contributor to *The Enquirer*. One of his essays 'On Verse and Poetry' (Enfiled, 1796) is said to have influenced Wordsworth's 'Preface to the Lyrical Ballads', which also celebrated the vernacular tongue.

The egalitarian streak within the Warrington Academy did not fully extend to girls but the daughter of another member of staff, John Aiken, did attend and was inspired to produce a similar anthology for girls. Anna Laetitia Barbour published *The Female Speaker* in 1816. Just over 25 years earlier, in 1789, Mary Wollstonecraft had also published *The Female Reader*. While not a dissenter herself, she had set up a school with help from the Newington Green Dissenters, a group which included the prominent dissenter Richard Price.

In her preface Wollstonecraft explains her debt to Enfield and while much of her justification for the volume may seem slightly conservative or modest for such a proto feminist nevertheless the link between thought, literature and its role in education is evident. For her thinking is more important than perfect elocution which 'may teach young people what to say; but will probably will prevent them ever learning to think'. (Wollstonecraft, 1789, 2003). For Wollstonecraft education was the key to empowerment.

What some theorists say

Having something to say

These two features, then, culture and language, the power to create and think, have possibly made English what it could be today. And this has made some sceptical about an examination system that seeks to constrain what pupils can show. To use a technical term it is 'construct under representation'. But English is not just about what can or cannot be written in an exam. It is also about how we progress in general, how we convey and interpret meaning. And if we think that English is a language art then pupils do not go in a straight line. They progress, but not according to a neat road map that can be charted and mapped out, or written up in a government document.

Elliot Eisner has written extensively on the arts within education and while he is not an English expert he still has much to say on the subject, which is relevant. Writing in 2002 in *The Arts and the Creation of Mind*, he grappled with what it means to create art. In it he writes, 'The linguistic act is the product of a linguistic imagination. The attitude required to use language of this kind is one that eludes the limiting constraints of literalism in perception and allows one to enter work emotionally' (Eisner, 2002, p. 88).

For him one has to, as it were, imagine the words on a page and that is something which cannot be constrained by 'literalism', the mechanics of writing and perceiving. Art, therefore, is about 'judgement in the absence of rules. Indeed, if there were rules for making such choices, judgement would not be necessary' (ibid., p. 77). Two things come together, the imagination and judgement. In some respects this sums up what English is about. When we write, we imagine, when we read, we judge. And yet the two can be combined as well. When we read we imagine other worlds, when we write, we judge our performance and alter it as we go along. Neither, however, are rule-bound.

He goes on to write, 'Work in the arts, unlike many other rule-governed forms of performance, always leave the door open to choice, and choice in this domain depends upon a sense of rightness' (ibid., p. 77). This, then, is what we encourage in pupils both through the reading that they do and also, crucially, through peer and self-assessment. When giving pupils pieces of work done by others we are encouraging them to consider the judgements and choices they have made and, ultimately, we are asking them whether they feel right.

Eisner's notion of judgement and too the sense of rightness depend upon an appreciation of the aesthetic and of artistry. 'Artistry', for Eisner,

> consists in having an idea worth expressing, the imaginative ability needed to conceive of how, the technical skills needed to work effectively with some material [in English the medium being words], and the sensibilities needed to make the delicate adjustments that will give the forms the moving qualities that the best of them possess. (ibid., p. 81)

All of these pupils engage in this when they peer assess. What is important, too, is that in peer assessment, although they will have to show 'technical skills' they will make 'delicate adjustments', rather than working to rule-bound formula of how the other person might improve. Progression, therefore, is a messy business. It does not have neat order. Instead one builds up a repertoire. Implicit within the term is the sense of a body of knowledge acquired through exposure, experimentation and practice. It connotes technique, artistry and interpretation but not an order in which they should be acquired. Above all it means that in English judgement is practised and criticism exercised.

As we shall see in later chapters, it is not upon Eisner, but Vygotsky, that much of the literature of peer assessment is based, and we will look at this in Chapter 4. For now it is worth considering the writing of John Dewey also.

Dewey was one of the major writers on progressive education but he also wrote at length on the nature of art including *Art as Experience*. In 1899, he wrote, 'There is all the difference in the world between having to say something and having something to say' (Dewey, 1899, p. 67), which in essence is what English teachers are trying to enable their pupils to do: to have something to say and say it to the best of their ability.

Dewey was not elitist in his view of culture. In fact Dewey was very keen that culture and aesthetics should not become elitist terms. He saw, 'The continuity of the aesthetic experience with the normal process of living' (Dewey, 2005, p. 9). To oversimplify his position slightly, Dewey believed that art arose out of a person's ability to shape the experiences they had, to give them or to perceive 'pattern and structure'.

In this respect he saw art as entirely about our ability to see things aesthetically, as about 'interaction between a live creature and some aspect of the world' (ibid., p. 45). But he saw more. Art, he claimed was also about people producing or creating works of art as well. For him artistry interwove these two elements – the ability to appreciate something as an audience and the ability to create or produce an artefact. The artist, then, is a person who can stand within an experience and outside it simultaneously. In so doing they have a dual perspective which enables them to position themselves both as the audience and creator at the same time. 'To be truly artistic,' Dewey wrote, 'a work must be aesthetic – that is framed for enjoyed receptive perception' (ibid., p. 49).

In their book *The Reader in the Writer*, (2002) Myra Barrs and Valerie Cook found something similar. Working with children, this time of primary school age, they noted that pupils read books and used them in their writing but not in any systematic way. In other words they did not follow the rules of any particular genre but rather played with ideas and expression to create new effects. Moreover reading books helped them have a sense that they were writing for someone. It gave them a sense of audience, that what they wrote was 'framed for enjoyed receptive perception' (ibid., p. 49).

Conclusion

So what then do we have? We have a subject which is all about judgement and choice. And this, in turn, means that it is about assessment. People who are good at English judge or assess almost everything. They assess whether the book they are reading is any good or whether the film they have just seen gripped them. They consider the style and form of what they have read and think about the visual grammar of a television programme. They may discuss a particular character or debate the central theme of a novel, but in doing so they are judging whether or not the writer had captured what it was they were trying to say. They examine adverts, even the back of cereal packets and what is more they assess what they themselves have written. Did they use the right word; was their expression cumbersome or that paragraph too long? All this they ask but they never stop assessing the quality of the text. People who are good at English assess.

Yet when asked to assess formally, English teachers baulk. For one thing they differ in their judgements. I may think that the novels of Jane Austen are divine, someone else may feel that they are the voice of a nineteenth-century woman talking of little else but local gossip. Then there is the problem that English, if it is to be considered an art, is not rule-bound and English teachers have a tendency to want to consider the whole of a piece rather than look at its constituent parts. This lands them in difficulties with most exam syllabuses. There is the problem, too, that most summative assessment does not capture all that a pupil does. They only select a small portion of what they can do And finally there is the problem that pupils are people who develop eccentrically. For many it is difficult constantly to assess a person's performance, always to think that there is something else they could do.

The question above all is how we put these two things together reliably? How do we get people, who assess everything they see to make judgements about pupils' work both formatively and summatively? Over the course of this book we hope to find out how some teachers have addressed this problem. For it should be remembered that understanding English as a language art enhances our standing within arts education in general. As Eisner wrote,

> Work in the arts is not only a way of creating performances and products; it is a way of creating our lives by expanding our consciousness, shaping our dispositions, satisfying our quest for meaning, establishing contact with others and sharing a culture. (Eisner, 2002, p. 3)

English and Postwar Experiments in Assessment

In a book apparently devoted to assessing English it would be tempting to address the totality of how English was assessed. But that would be a different book. We will look instead at what might be called case studies but which are in fact just examples of how English teachers have sought to come to terms with assessment in their subject. In this chapter, we will look in particular, at how, between the Butler Education Act of 1944 and the Education Reform Act of 1988, English teachers themselves tried to suggest ways in which their subject might be assessed. For what is interesting is that they tried to achieve reform of the system by a kind of bottom up process by which they attempted to influence the exam boards, who, in turn, altered what they did. What we will see, in particular, is an attempt to judge English more holistically rather than in a piecemeal way.

The first set of examples we will look at all come from London, the second from the Joint Matriculation Board (JMB) in Manchester. The London Association of the Teachers of English (LATE) was founded in 1947, 16 years before the national organization, NATE, was conceived, and was formed both as an aid to English teachers but also to undertake research into particular areas of English teaching. LATE was closely associated with the Institute of Education and James Britton. Later the association became so closely identified with people at the Institute that it developed into something known as the London School of English. Commentators, on the development of English, such as Ball or Goodson (1990) have used this to mark out London's opposition to the Cambridge School, which was based on the work, among others, of F. R. Leavis. The London School looked at the everyday language that children used and for some this has meant that it was very language based. Peter Abbs (1982), has for example, called it 'socio-linguistic' in its orientation.

> The sociolinguists were out demonstrate that the truth was not simply 'out there' to be imprinted on the passive mind of the child; but that it was made through individual attempts to actively formulate meaning. (ibid., p. 19)

James Britton and LATE

The Barnet Syllabus

But whatever its leanings, very early on, within five years of its inception, LATE, were beginning to ask questions about how children were assessed. They campaigned for a new syllabus for the English Language General Certificate in Education Ordinary-level. The final syllabus, which was accepted in 1955, became known as the Barnet syllabus, because in the end only one school, Queen Elizabeth Girls, in Barnet, actually took the exam.

They began their examination with the O-level, which was designed for grammar school children, around 20 per cent of pupils. The 1944 Education Act had begun to change the nature of pupils who were entering grammar school. To begin with the school leaving age had risen from 14 to 15, which would not especially affect schools but it was possible to enter the examination early. Anybody thinking of leaving at 15 could be entered for the exam but take it in the fourth, rather than the fifth year of secondary school. In addition, the majority of people who went to grammar schools, in traditional class terms, were either the top end of the working class or lower middle class. For the average English teacher this meant that the O-Level exam, as it was, could be seen as elitist. LATE was keen that the O-level should suit its main clientele rather then some abstruse group of children who they themselves did not teach. Writing in 1952, they said,

> The sort of children the examiners had in mind were children who visited pen friends abroad, who were chairman of school dramatic clubs, and who arranged

private dances. Was this symptomatic of the examiners 'sympathy' with children? (LATE, 1952, cited in Gibbons, 2009, p. 21)

This was not the kind of person they had in front of them. In the 1951 conference they looked at the Literature and Language O-levels and as a result formed a sub-committee, which was to examine them more closely. What is interesting about the committee and the subsequent work which they did, is that at no point did they think of abandoning the formal GCE, rather, they thought about altering it only. Ten years later, and in another part of the country, as we shall see, the outcome was, in some respects, far more radical as they were proposing getting rid of the formal exam altogether. LATE were, however, trying to get through a loophole in the exam board, which said that a school or group of schools could, 'submit to the Board an alternative syllabus for approval, which could then be used as the examination for their children in preference to the Board's standard paper' (Gibbons, 2009, p. 21).

No such considerations exist like this any more, as we shall see in the next chapter, but then, significantly, the Boards did allow a degree of flexibility and this was important. For what LATE were trying to do was have their everyday teaching, and the linguistic demands of their pupils, somehow reflected in the final exam they took. James Britton, writing in 1955, after the London Board had been awarded the right to LATE's alternative syllabus, wrote:

> It seems to me that, in principle, there ought not to be any better way of preparing a pupil for examination than good teaching: and that the examining authorities ought to recognize the principle and make themselves responsible for providing an examination which as nearly as possible satisfies it. . . . One effect of the English language paper is to encourage training in certain restricted techniques at the expense of more broadly based language teaching. (Britton, 1955, cited in Gibbons, ibid., p. 22)

In this he is characteristic, as we shall see, of the numerous complaints English teachers have made of formal exams – that they do not characterize the diversity of experience that goes on in the English classroom. Although the LATE syllabus was not that different from the one on offer it did differ in certain crucial respects. Perhaps the main difference came in the way they merged literature and language, particularly in the comprehension, where it made no difference as to whether the passage chosen for analysis was a literary or non-literary text. (In fact they asked pupils to respond to both types of text.)

This played a central role in how LATE saw English. In October 1952 they held a conference under the title *English: Two subjects or one*. *The Guardian* newspaper commenting on the outcomes of the conference said that the teacher was responsible 'to the child rather than to the literature' (*Guardian*, cited in ibid., p. 23). What mattered was how the child saw, responded to and created language rather than having a set view of language, often via literary texts, imposed upon them. Simon Gibbons, writing about the syllabus as a whole says that it does 'show significant moves towards the kind of assessment of "language in operation" that would be fundamental to future developments in what has since become termed "London English"' (ibid., p. 28).

The meaning and marking of imaginative compositions

Central also to London English was what was then called composition. Published a year before LATE began looking at exam syllabuses was the *Report on the Meaning and Marking of Imaginative Compositions* (Britton, 1950). This also looked at how English might be assessed more holistically. A group of people in LATE wanted to know how they could mark English essays more reliably. In the end seven individuals took part in the experiment. They began by thinking of the criteria they used to mark compositions. Although he does not give the full list of everyone's ideas Britton marks out those which he thinks important. So for one he puts,

> Quality of imagination shown in detail (number, variety, value of idea).
> Structure of a sentence.
> Precision in language.
> Total effect. (ibid., p. 1)

And another

> Imaginative conception (what the writer has made for himself from the material given him).
> Literary technique. Extent to which his mastery of vocabulary, sentence structure, etc. enables him to express his imaginative conception in words.
> Practical equipment – spelling, punctuation, handwriting. (ibid., p. 1)

In the end they 'selected two items which, between them, seemed to cover the greater part of what we meant by imaginative composition. These were a) pictorial quality and b) creativeness' (ibid., p. 2). This is an interesting choice given that the criteria which he cites did not include either. In fact they chose criteria which are quite closely allied with the current Assessing Pupils' Progress (APP), which we shall look at in the next chapter and Chapter 6. Pictorial quality, on the other hand, conveys the idea that someone who writes composition portrays an image in words, as well as describing something in detail. To use the metaphor – they paint a picture. Creativeness, the other criterion, is a laden term. Later on in the report it is defined thus: 'To what extent is what the writer has written new, original, individual? (Creativeness)' (ibid., p. 2). In a way this begs certain questions. Do you have to be individual to be original? Is being new different from being original? Do you have to be all three before you are considered creative and are there more criteria that would fit just as well?

When it came to the marking of pupils' essays it was found that they did indeed interpret the criteria differently. The same essays came back with very different grades. 'In spite therefore of our most careful preparation (months of discussion) we clearly did not agree on the qualities required of good imaginative composition' (ibid., p. 3). This then became the focus of further research. When they had first decided to look at pupil essays they had asked children to write for an hour. Now they asked them to write a 100-word piece and changed the criteria again. This time they asked for:

1) General impression (By your own personal method; by impression rather than by analysis in search of particular characteristics).
2) To what extent can the reader experience what is presented (i.e. see, feel, hear etc.).
3) Originality of ideas. To what extent is the writer's view of the subject distinctive (i.e. as compared with the ideas of the group as a whole.).
4) Feeling for words. To what degree does the writer use words a) strikingly AND b) effectively?

In some respects the items two and three are the same as was asked for before, only with the second criterion they have asked for more than just the pictorial, they have asked for other senses like 'feel' and 'hear'. They have asked too for 'originality' as opposed to 'creativity' but given that originality was specified under the heading creativity it is similar. This time, however, they are asked for 'distinctiveness' from their fellow writers. In this respect originality is a lesser demand given that they only have to be distinctive from their peers. What are new are the first and fourth criteria – 'feeling for words' and 'general impression'. This is the first time Britton and the LATE team ask markers to assess for impression. What is important is that they are not to mark by 'analysis in search of particular characteristics'. In another way they are being asked for their gut feeling.

Even with the new set of criteria, however, the assessors still disagreed. What the LATE team was required to do was to mark the short pieces separately for each individual criterion. So, for example, they marked first for impression, then for what was presented, third for originality and so on. They also wanted to prevent something called the 'halo effect'. This was where one set of criterion on a piece of work influenced the marking of another piece of work. In order to prevent this the candidates' work was rendered anonymous and the order was discontinuous, in other words assessors didn't mark similar work one after the other but different kinds of work. They were also asked to repeat mark certain compositions to see if their marking had changed between one session and the next. The re-marking of work for different criteria is again, as we shall see in Chapters 3 and 6, not unlike some people's interpretation of APP, in that they were trying to segment children's writing into categories.

The grades were put through an elaborate factor analysis to see if anything else could be elicited from the results. It is interesting that for an apparently subjective exercise – marking essays – Britton chose to do such quantitative work. Having said this he found that despite differences in how they interpreted the compositions the assessors were reliable.

Multiple marking of compositions

Still interested, a decade and a half later, in how one could make English markers more reliable and valid, Britton held an enquiry into examination marking yet again. He appears to have abandoned looking at a variety of criteria in an APP type fashion, however, and is much more interested in the markers' general impression. What is interesting to note, is that he still, it would seem, had faith that a timed test was legitimate. At the time he was carrying out his experiment, the JMB, as we shall see, had already moved towards a course-based exam, as had the CSE Boards with a mode three qualification. Britton was still concerned, that teachers' judgements were unreliable because they differed so much in what they thought about English but he thought that they were more likely to be reliable than the method he called 'analytic marking'.

In this trial, on actual O-level papers, he compared scripts, which had been marked by board examiners, with what he now called 'rapid impression markers'. Each script was marked both by a board examiner and then separately by a team of four people. Three marked the script impressionistically and one marked for technical accuracy. These markers were taken from all over the country and were asked to time how long it took them to assess the papers. This was done to show that impression marking was done more quickly than the traditional form of examination marking. A sample of the scripts was then sent to the board examiner and members of the team about six weeks later so that the reliability could be assessed. The impression markers were also asked to write 'brief notes on the criteria upon which they had based their assessments' (Britton, 1964, p. 19).

Britton analysed these 'brief notes' when considering the validity of the experiment and the results are quite revealing as to what the examiners saw was good in a piece. He quotes that they felt the 'sincerity' and 'involvement' of the writing as well as the 'real feeling' and 'real experience'. This in a way validates the London School's aim that pupils should write out of their own experience. They also, however, talked about the organization of the piece and used phrases such as 'the general shape' and, too, 'the aesthetic form'. Here, then, they are using phrases which are talking about the artistic form of the piece. Britton went on to classify the markers' comments in descending order of importance. These were 'a) involvement, b) organization, c) mechanical accuracy' (ibid., p. 23). The section on mechanical accuracy was given little overall weight by the markers, within the general impression of the piece, but it was mentioned.

Britton was interested in the general overlap of comments given by these assessors in their impression marking because they were marking essays on such different topics. He had organized it so that a minority of pupils were asked to write two selected essays, as opposed to one, choosing from ten different topics. These included such titles as a single word like 'Colour', a descriptive piece, an imaginative piece, an autobiographical piece or an argument. It is clear he believed, given the variety of essays, the markers would have different reactions to the different types but they did not. The comments on one type of essay were very similar to those of another. When asked, therefore, about a piece of writing, it would seem that there was something about an 'impression' that remained the same for English teachers.

What did alter slightly was the pupils' individual attempts at the type of essay. In this respect he found it better that they should be asked to do more than one type of writing, as this would give a fairer reflection of their ability in English. In fact 'fairness' is a word that is repeated quite often throughout the report. He felt that the traditional exam was unfair to many pupils. Indeed as a result of the experiment he was able to conclude that,

> The system of multiple marking employed in this experiment, used to mark essay scripts written in a public examination of a GCE Board, gave a greater reliability

and validity than the system of marking of that Board, rigorous though it was. (ibid., p. 27)

Writing nearly 25 years on he was still convinced that the type of multiple impression marking advocated was best. 'The upshot of the experiment was to indicate that parcelling out scripts to examiners is a considerably less reliable process than parcelling them out to teams of three rapid impression markers' (Britton and Martin, 1989, p. 2). They also found it more accurate than the traditional 'very careful analytic marking system' (ibid., pp. 2–3).

In this he contrasts greatly with the exam boards of today which, like their former incarnations, favour, quite heavily, a more analytic form of marking. Even coursework must be heavily annotated. The Qualifications, Curriculum Development Authority also prefer exams to have an atomistic and fragmented marking system rather than one which takes a holistic approach this, despite Britton's finding that impressionistic marking is more reliable.

Nevertheless, despite criticizing the exam board system in 1964, he still found an examination, of a sort, preferable to the increased tendency towards coursework assessment. This may be in part because he still found straight teacher assessment too unreliable a method of assessing pupils' work. Indeed he even criticized the work of Petch, who, as we shall see, was director of the research unit at JMB and was one of the people involved in carrying out research into 100 per cent coursework. He also queried Certificate of Secondary Examinations (CSE), which was also working on teacher assessment.

Joint Matriculation Board[1]

The JMB decided to follow a course that was somewhat different from the LATE, or certainly James Britton. They decided to go for a pattern that was more like the CSE mode 3 exams , which were just beginning to get going in the early 60s. What is interesting is that the experiment they embarked on was sponsored for the first three years by the Department of Education and Science and in its last year by the Schools Council. It seems that the DES were not wholly unsympathetic to finding alternative forms of examination, or at least did not mind investigating them. The JMB started work on 100 per cent coursework in 1964 but their concern over the syllabus had been going for some time. In an interim report written in 1965, the then Chairman of the JMB, wrote, 'The complicated problems arising from examining English

Language have been the concern of the Joint Matriculation Board, among many others, for a long time' (Wilson, in Hewitt and Gordon, 1965, p. 1). In fact the JMB and the University of Durham, which was also taking part in the experiment, had been interested in what they were doing in London in the 50s and had asked, for example, for the draft syllabus written by LATE in 1952 (Gibbons, 2009). What is worth noting is that in justification of the new alternative syllabus they wrote,

> The GCE O-level examination in English language is under bitter criticism as conducive to dull and cramped teaching and to crabbed rote learning and practice. The lively interest which should be aroused by learning to read and write English is killed, so it is asserted, by the need to prepare for writing stereotyped answers. (Wilson, 1965, p. 1)

The language used to describe the exam is strong. The criticism is 'bitter'. The tasks are 'dull'. They use the words 'cramped' and 'crabbed' which are not only harsh but have an alliterative, almost onomatopoeic, effect which builds towards the idea of 'rote learning'. Any enjoyment, which should be 'aroused', is 'killed'. There is literally no life when pupils prepare 'stereotyped answers'. As we have seen, the language which James Britton used explained what was potentially wrong with the system, 'One effect of the English language paper is to encourage training in certain restricted techniques at the expense of more broadly based language teaching' (Britton, 1955). Ten years on, the JMB are using a much more powerful language almost to decry what they think is wrong with the exam.

Their unprecedented attack on the system left them, however, with a question.

> But if the teacher of English is to be free to teach his pupils English as he thinks he should teach them without regard to traditional examination, how can the examining board, whose *testamur* at the end of the course is required, be assured that by the end of the course those pupils have benefitted from this untrammelled teaching and learning to an extent which merits an O-level pass in English. (ibid., p. 1)

This then is the point of the experiment: to ensure that that almost romantic term, 'untrammelled teaching' should succeed. In all the criticisms of exam teaching one gets the impression that English should be a subject which enjoys vistas, not be forced down narrow back streets. All the words which explain the exams are constraining from Britton's 'restricted' to the JMBs 'cramped' and 'crabbed'. In saying that the teaching should be 'untrammelled' it indicates that pupils should be taken down paths untravelled before. In this they are asking for originality rather than 'stereotyped answers'. The problem is how you assess this.

Instead of having an exam with multiple markers, as Britton had done, however, the JMB were going to have a system where pupils submitted five pieces of coursework completed in the final year of the exam. Although the pupils' work was not marked multiple examiners as in the case of the London trials, in effect many of the candidates work was marked several times. All folders had to be marked by the teacher and then a grade agreed on by the school. In order to do this at least some of the work had to be re-marked. A sample was then sent off to a moderator. Thus is meant that the work was read at least three times.

The way they chose the moderators was significant. Throughout the year they had trial marking meetings. In the first instance this meant schools bringing along candidates' work which the rest of the participating schools marked as well. The board then located those teachers whose grading was most closely allied to the group as a whole. These moderators did not visit the schools but were given samples of the work completed by a school. In the event, 'High correlations between schools and moderators were achieved' (ibid., p. 10). This process, for finding what eventually became know as Review Panel members, was retained and we shall look at the final system of assessment which was 'gradually modified over the years', (Smith, 1978, p. 4) shortly. For now it is worth looking at the main thrust of what they found.

In the first place, although all the teachers involved in the project disliked 'external examinations' and preferred pupils to be assessed by 'continuous writing', it is doubtful whether the 'score or so of teachers who attended the meetings would all subscribe to a declaration of intent and interests couched in less general terms' (Hewitt and Gordon, 1965, p. 12). In other words their views of English were very different despite their unified displeasure at exams. '"Like-minded" is not a description that we would apply to the group' (ibid., p. 12). Far from finding this problematic, however, this was seen as a potential asset. A 'degree of adaptability is perhaps an a more important criterion for the formation of such groups' (ibid., p. 12). All then that was important was that they were adaptable, not that they all felt the same way about English. Something which had been seen as a difficulty, then, that English teachers did not all agree as to what the subject was, could become an advantage. For apart from anything else, although they did not agree with what the subject was, they did agree in how it should be assessed. In this way a kind of consensus, from disparate views, of grading was reached.

A cordial dislike of exams, however, continued into the next report, this time written by Petch.

> In sum among teachers co-operating with the board in this experiment the opinion is widely held that all the tests normally set in traditional English Language papers go directly counter to what they think is the proper function of teachers in secondary schools, namely 'to encourage the pupil through reading, more and more about himself and the nature of his human and physical environment, and in speech and writing to make statements about relationships that are truly interesting'. (Petch, 1967, p. 5)

The implied criticism of the English Language exam then is that it does not produce anything 'truly interesting'. Petch might have used the descriptions found in the previous report, to describe the O-level – writing that is 'dull' and 'cramped' and 'crabbed'.

In the final report, written in 1970, it was found that the results achieved at coursework were somewhat better than those acquired through the 'traditional English Language papers'. 'The teachers were satisfied that the high pass percentage was justified and that the high standard of work was the result of the freedom established by the scheme for both teachers and pupils.' (Rooke and Hewitt, 1970, p. 9). This too is telling. 'Freedom' has come for both pupils and teachers. Teachers, because they can teach how they like and for pupils because, presumably they learn better and what they learn is properly assessed. In a way this is a comment on the increased validity of the exam.

In 1978, a year after the JMB had introduced the exam nationally, they wrote another pamphlet entitled *JMB Experience of Moderation of Internal Assessment*. In this they wrote again on the benefits of coursework as opposed to terminal examinations.

> It is more likely, however, that internal assessment is proposed because of a conviction that it is a more valid way of assessing the attributes or the skills which are involved. Increased validity could result for two reasons: first because the assessment of skills concerned may be difficult or impossible to achieve by external examination and second, because assessment on a single occasion may be a totally inadequate test of a candidate's overall competence. (Smith, 1978, p. 5)

This sounds very like the complaints that would come about later on the abolition of coursework General Certificate in Secondary Education (GSCE) and the Sats. The first is also very reminiscent of the Macnamara Fallacy. Charles Handy in his book *The Empty Raincoat* cites it thus:

> The first step is to measure whatever can be easily measured. This is OK as far as it goes. The second is to disregard that which can't be easily measured or to give it arbitrary quantitative value. This is artificial and misleading. The third step is to presume that what can't be measured easily really isn't important. This is blindness. The fourth step is to say that what can't be easily measured really doesn't exist. This is suicide. (Handy, 1995, p. 219)

What the teachers were in effect saying was that terminal exams are a possibly suicidal form of measurement because they only assess what is easy to assess and ignore, at best, or at worst consider non-existent, all those attributes which can only be assessed throughout the course of a year.

The validity of an assessment, however, is dependent on its reliability too, and here we come back to the method of marking coursework-based exams. Although, as we have seen, the system of choosing moderators remained largely the same, the procedures for assessment did change slightly, and they are worth noting in full.

To begin with the JMB and its successor, the Northern Examination Association Board (NEAB), demanded that all teachers with examination classes had to assess, bi-annually, trial marking material, consisting of folders of work of candidates from the previous year. As early as 1970 Rooke and Hewitt, working for the JMB, note, 'Experience has shown that it is essential for groups to meet together to discuss the results of trial marking and procedures for assessment.' (Rooke and Hewitt, 1970, p. 14.). They go on to recommend that, on the extension of the scheme, 'Provision must therefore be made for groups to meet for discussion' (ibid., p. 14).

The folders always contained one or two candidate's work that were difficult to assess, for example a C/D borderline. All teachers marked these folders blind then met with the rest of the department in order that a school grade could be decided. The individual scores and the school's agreed grades were sent back to the board. A standardization meeting was then held by the board, in which the grades, agreed by a Review Panel, were given out. The Review Panel was made up of practicing teachers, who, as with the original experiment, had been chosen for the accuracy of their assessments, through the trial marking.

The system by which the actual work of pupils was assessed was similarly rigorous. To ensure the reliability of these judgements checks and double checks were introduced. All candidates were marked both by their own teacher and another member of department. Where there was any disagreement, or when the candidate was on the borderline between two grades, their folder was submitted for scrutiny by the whole department.

The whole school entry was then moderated to ensure that the candidates' work was placed in the correct rank order, from grade A to U, before sending them to the exam board. Here the work was moderated by a member of the Review Panel. All Review Panel members worked with partners. When one panel member moderated a school's entry, the other checked their judgement. The Review Panel members had the power to alter a school's grades, either up or down, if they felt that they had placed more than 50 per cent of the candidates on the wrong grade. A 'C' could become a 'D' or a 'B' an 'A'. (The rank order of individual candidates could be changed only when the Review Panel members felt that an individual candidate had been wrongly graded by at least two complete grades.) The work of the vast majority of candidates was, therefore, read by at least five different English teachers before a final grade was awarded. One final check was built into the system. A sample of the cohort was sent to an Inter School Assessor. This teacher marked the entry blind and then sent their grades to the Review Panel. Again if there were any serious discrepancy between the Assessors' grades and the school's, the panel members would moderate the school's entry.

The exam boards returned all coursework to the schools, after they had been externally moderated, with comments on any adjustments that had been made as well as on the quality of the work. In this way the whole process of exam board's decisions and moderations was entirely made by ordinary teachers whose own pupils were being examined. Moreover, a national network began to develop where the teachers were firmly in charge, but learning constantly from the dialogues that were created by the process.

Although, as we shall see in the next chapter, 100 per cent coursework exams were abandoned, the NEAB which later became the Associated Qualifications Authority (AQA), has approximately 75 per cent of the total cohort completing GCSE. What is more, although only 20 per cent of the exam is written coursework they still send out trial marking once a year for schools to do.

Guild knowledge

What neither James Britton and LATE, or the JMB give, however, is any indication of how English teachers arrived at the grades that they gave pupils. Britton's impression marking is one thing, saying how you arrive at that impression is quite another. This is where the work of Royce Sadler comes in. In 1989 he wrote a seminal article in which he talked, among other things, about 'guild knowledge'. In a way, what James Britton called impression marking was similar to Sadler's guild knowledge. Sadler said that teachers had a guild knowledge, which they could not necessarily articulate, but which they shared with others in their profession. He suggests, that way the in which teachers cope with the multiplicity of variables confronting them, when marking an essay, for example, is by making what he calls 'qualitative judgements' about pupils' work. A teacher of English, therefore, has a guild knowledge of what makes a good essay. Significantly he did not say anything about the differences of point of view of a subject that say an English teacher might have with another English teacher.

What was important in teaching was that in some way the teacher imparted this knowledge to the pupil. But he admits, 'How to draw the concept of excellence out of the heads of teachers, give it some external formulation, and make it available to the learner, is a non trivial problem' (ibid, p. 127). As we shall in later chapters this is important in formative assessment but for now it is worth pursuing a bit further what Sadler has to say. Essentially, he argues, that criteria are unhelpful in improving performance. 'For complex phenomena, use of a fixed set of criteria (and therefore the analytic approach) is potentially limiting' (Sadler, 1989, p. 132). Instead he argues for what he calls 'configurational assessment' which he explains 'do[es] not require the specification of all the criteria in advance, neither do they assume operational independence among the criteria' (ibid.).

One reason he appears to give for the interrelatedness of criteria, and therefore the difficulty, not to say impossibility of separating them out, is because,

> The greater the divergence in outcomes which can be regarded as acceptable, the more likely it is that a variety of ways can be devised to alter the gap between actual and reference levels, and therefore the less likely it is that information about the gap will in itself suggest a remedial action. (ibid., p. 139)

In other words if a child writes a descriptive piece there are any number of ways it could be improved. Identifying, for example, the increased use of complex sentences among higher achieving pupils, and so teaching that element explicitly, is insufficient. Only with surface features such as spelling and punctuation is such a simple procedure possible. Moreover, he goes on to argue that with extended writing,

> Any attempt to mechanise such educational activities and creative efforts [as for example with ILS software packages] is unlikely to be successful because of the large number of variables involved, the intense relationship existing among them, and their essential fuzziness. (ibid., p. 140)

What Sadler calls 'their essential fuzziness' and perhaps James Britton calls an impression, for others is the term 'judgement'. Protherough, Atkinson and Fawcett, when talking about assessment, write, 'In the end, grade descriptions for English have to be matters of judgement and not of objective fact, and developing this judgement is one of the skills that young English teachers have to acquire' (Protherough, Atkinson and Fawcett, 1989, p. 31). In other words the guild knowledge which Sadler speaks of is acquired over time. The question then becomes – how do people gain this sense of judgement or guild knowledge?

A community of interpreters

It is here that the work of Dylan Wiliam is significant (see Wiliam, 1994, 1996, 1998) and, from the point of view of formative assessment, develops the work of Sadler, in that his research suggests the means or mechanism by which teachers acquire the ability to make reliable qualitative judgements. He describes this as 'construct referencing'. Neither norm referencing, nor criteria referencing in its strictest sense, construct referencing has elements of both and something else besides. In essence, when English teachers award a grade to a piece of work, or a folder, they are using a construct of what they think that grade looks like, based on their previous encounters with work of a similar standard – very like Britton's impression marking.

Wiliam argues that teacher's understanding of the construct is honed by considering and discussing borderline cases and argues that the procedures instituted by the examination boards created what he describes as a 'community of interpreters'. We have seen that this was particularly strong element in the way that JMB organized events, including the regular trial marking. Trial marking, along with the network of local consortia, meant that teachers were engaged in a constant debate, with other practitioners from a variety of different schools, about levels of achievement in pupils' work. In this way a professional discourse began to emerge. The annual moderation of candidates' folders meant that lessons learned in the abstract, through trial marking, were applied to the pupils in your school. What had emerged from the apparently mundane activity of marking was a shared meaning among a community of interpreters or what Sadler might describe as 'guild knowledge'. As Wiliams points out:

> The innovative feature of such assessment is that no attempt is made to prescribe learning outcomes. In that it is defined at all, it is defined simply as the consensus of the teachers making the assessments. The assessment is not objective, in that there are no objective criteria for a student to satisfy . . . the assessment system relies on the existence of a construct (of what it means to be competent in a particular domain) being shared by a community of interpreters. (Wiliam, 1998, p. 6)

Observation of these standardization, or trial marking, meetings illustrate this well (see Marshall, 2000). At school level teachers, while constantly bemoaning the shortcomings of criteria, do refer to them in order to support their judgements. Yet the way in which they do so is significant. The most typical pattern involves one teacher reading aloud a section of a candidate's work and then referring to the criteria to which they think this applies. These interjections are, however, frequently countermanded by another teacher repeating the process with another piece of text and the relevant criterion to refute the first teacher's assertion. To this extent these discussions are clear evidence of the way in which, as Wiliam's (1998) paper suggests, it is the interpretation of evidence that is crucial rather than the criterion descriptors themselves.

But what they also illustrate is that some teachers are better at assessing than others. Assessment is a skill like any other part of teaching. Teachers disagree as to what is good or bad but what is important is that this is not based on what particular view of English they happen to hold but on how good they are at assessing the candidates' work (Marshall, 2000, 2001). In other words, some teachers appear to 'get' the construct better than others. This is why, for example, the JMB's practice of selecting Review Panel members from the consistency of their trial marking was beneficial. It reinforced a particular and consistent view of what a grade was, reinforced over time. And this in turn made the way pupils were assessed more reliable.

Conclusion

As we shall see in later chapters this sense of a guild knowledge affects the way in which English teachers adopted assessment for learning including peer review, self-assessment and exemplar material of work at different grades. All of these are, in some ways, the teacher's attempts to communicate their knowledge or judgement about English to the pupils that they teach. The key to understanding why such practices might more readily recommend themselves in the English classroom is the nature of the subject discipline.

For, in some respects, assessment lies at the heart of the subject of English. When we read a piece of work we are judging it. When we write, we analyse what we have written and so judge it again. But on both occasions we are doing so through the interpretation of the evidence we have in front of us rather than through the strict application of criteria. Or rather we are calling upon a whole repertoire of criteria and judging to see which one is apt for this particular piece of writing. To quote Sadler once more, in looking at writing, be it our own or someone else's there are a, 'large number of variables involved' which have an 'essential fuzziness'.

To summarize, it may be, therefore, that English teachers' apparent distrust of 'analytic' forms of assessment arises from the nature of the discipline. What the case studies show us is that there has always been an attempt to match English teachers' view of the subject with the way it has been assessed. From the 1950s onwards this was an organic, bottom up approach where boards and teachers discussed the best way to assess the subject. As we shall see in the next chapter, all this changed with the Education Reform Act of 1988 and the introduction of the National Curriculum the following year.

Note

1. Official acknowledgement is made to the Joint Matriculation Board for allowing access to confidential material. The JMB does not necessarily accept the views expressed in this chapter.

3 Post 1989 in England, Wales and Scotland

Curriculum testing in England and Wales

When the national curriculum, for England and Wales, arrived in 1989 all this changed completely. By 1991 it was no longer possible to do any experimentation with the amount of coursework to be done at either GCSE or A-level. For in June of that year John Major, then Prime Minister, announced, at an after dinner speech of the Centre for Policy studies, that no more than 20 per cent of examinations could be done through coursework. In November Ken Clarke, the Secretary of State for Education, did extend this limit slightly when he gave the new criteria for English and English Literature GSCE. 40 per cent of English was to be coursework and 30 per cent Literature but it was still significantly less than the 100 per cent which had been allowed. From this point onwards the amount of coursework was determined by central government; no exam board could determine how much was to be done. It was this decision, along with the introduction of testing in the national curriculum, that in all probability caused the Sats boycott of 1993 and 1994 (Baker, 1994), for English teachers led the way in refusing to do them.

Initially, in the national curriculum, there were ten levels of achievement, each one being divided up into Statements of Attainment. A pupil would progress throughout their school career along these levels and at certain key stages – 7, 11 and 14 – they would receive a measure of how they had done. The average 7-year-old was expected to be a level 2, 11-year-old, level 4 and a 14-year-old, level 5. The Task Group on Assessment and Testing (TGAT) report, chaired by Professor Paul Black, had suggested that there were to be two forms of assessment at each of the three key stages – teacher assessment and a test. They had not specified what form the test or task should take.

The fact that there were to be two indicators of a pupil's progress was a problem to many English teachers but the tasks that were to be set for KS3 English were proving slightly better than was expected. The Consortium for Assessment and Testing in Schools (CATS) was at the time piloting the proposed tasks, which were to be marked by the teachers themselves. These tasks took place over a period of time, approximately three lessons, so there was room for redrafting work built into the assignment. Tasks included, for example, a set of Dore pictures of Coleridge's *The Ancient Mariner*. Teachers were encouraged to teach as normally as possible during these lessons so that the atmosphere did not become tense or too exam like.

Moreover, they were told when marking them, that they were not to consider the Statements of Attainment separately but to think of the levels holistically, not to wonder whether a child had reached a statement individually but to ask broadly whether or not they had achieved, say, a level 5. Most important of all, the CATS team worked out an equivalence to GCSE in the marking. A level 5 was a 'D' at GCSE, a level 6, a 'C' and so on. This meant that the teachers, already used to marking GCSEs, found it relatively unproblematic to convert this knowledge into levels. Although they would rather not have had to do these tasks at all, and rely simply on teacher assessment, teachers felt that they still contained something that was like the English they believed in.

While the pilots for the key stage three tests were going quite well, then, in English at least, the exams for 7-year-olds were a disaster, and the whole testing regime ground to a halt. The Conservative government had, in its infinite wisdom, decided to start the testing regime with 7-year-olds. In the summer of 1991, all 7-year-olds in England and Wales were assessed by their teachers. Particularly bad were the science tests, where children had to keep notes on whether or not items floated or sank. The sea of illegible, damp paper brought about ferocious comment in the press and may indirectly have explained John Major's tirade against coursework. The CATs consortium was sacked and a new contract was issued, this time to the Northern Examinations and Assessment Board (NEAB). The NEAB, however, only held the contract for a year. After a Tory victory in the general election of 1992, John Patten, the new Secretary of State, over the course of the summer holidays, put UCLES, (now Cambridge Assessment) with a history of overseas examining in charge of the tests.

Sats boycott

Instead of tasks, which pupils were asked to do over a period of time, pencil and paper tests were introduced. Pupils' comprehension was to be tested by multiple-choice questions: an anthology of literature and, for the first time, a Shakespeare play were also added to the items to be assessed.

What is interesting is the type of response to the tests, and the teaching required for them, when teachers eventually saw them. 'A more didactic approach/More time spent on "bitesize" (superficial) responses to literature (implying a "right" answer)/Less time to develop individual responses' (Cooper and Davies, 1993, p. 566). All these indicate a very different approach to the way in which teachers felt they organized their classrooms at the time. They felt that they would have to teach to the test, to be more 'didactic' which in turn would mean fewer 'individual responses'. Above all they believed that they would have to encourage students to give the 'right' answer, something which is directly opposed to an arts view of literature.

Mike Lloyd, a teacher from Birmingham, was at the time campaigning to keep 100 per cent coursework. Known as the Save English Course work Campaign, Lloyd petitioned 4000 schools (almost all the secondary schools in the country), both independent and maintained, and received an 85 per cent return. Of this 85 per cent, 95 per cent wanted no more than 20 per cent timed testing (Lloyd, 1994, 1997) a precise reversal of John Major's dictat. Lloyd's campaign, however, was to prove totally unsuccessful.

The London Association of the Teachers of English (LATE), who had surveyed all the secondary schools in England, found that English teachers would boycott the Sats if 500 schools joined them. In November 1992, at a decisive meeting at the English and Media Centre in London, they voted unanimously to boycott the Sats. It wasn't until the following Easter at the NAS/UWT and NUT conferences that the unions officially came on board.

After the boycott

The boycott only lasted for two years and in 1995 a new curriculum, along with new tests, came on board. The Sats had only changed marginally since the boycott. There were no more multiple-choice questions and the anthology had gone too but Shakespeare remained. The biggest difference was that now they were to be externally assessed rather than by the pupils' classroom teachers. This was because the NAS/UWT had said, as part of their campaign against the Sats, that they caused too much extra work for teachers. Given that they had changed beyond recognition from the days of the CATs consortium, this was not a major complaint, but a major cause of dissatisfaction ever after was that teachers did not believe that the results accurately reflected pupil ability. In the main this was to do with the validity of test but it did have something to do with the marking of the test also.

The London Association for the Teaching of English collected many of the objections that teachers felt about doing the so-called Sats exam. The first report was actually collated during the national boycott; the second after pupils had done them for one year. They were called *Voices from the classroom* (1993) and *The real cost of SATs* (1995). As one teacher wrote in the in the second booklet:

> The Sats have a negative influence on the curriculum because they narrow and limit what can be done. They tend to eliminate creativity and imagination in both the teachers and the student. Instead we are told what to do, what play to read, and what scenes will be examined. (LATE, 1995, p. 31)

While these are just anecdotal accounts, the teaching unions also carried out surveys of teacher opinion. The National Union of Teachers (NUT) completed a questionnaire of secondary English, maths and science in the summer of 1995 (Close, Furlong and Swain, 1995). It asked to what extent teachers felt the tests had altered their practice and also to what extent they used past papers. By far the highest number to believe that their practice was being affected were English teachers. They felt that the potential for variety of responses posed a threat which needed to be circumscribed by close attention to the likeliest answers. They could no longer encourage a wide range of responses to a text.

Research carried out by the Association of Teachers and Lecturers (ATL, 1996), published the following year, found that nearly three-quarters of English teachers felt they had been 'teaching to the test more than was reasonable'

(ATL, p. 16) as opposed to just over a quarter of maths teachers and almost a fifth of science teachers. In fact, the figures also showed that while English teachers had become increasingly frustrated with the distorting effect of the tests, science and maths teachers were accommodating more easily. The figure of dissatisfaction for English teachers stood at just over half, compared with over around two-fifths of maths teachers and a fifth of science teachers. Nearly 80 per cent of English teachers felt that 'the tests [had] narrowed the curriculum' (ATL, p. 12).

Arguments about the validity of the tests raged throughout their 14 years on the statute books. Every summer the papers were furnished with complaints that the Sats had failed to show the ability of pupils, particularly the most able; that they often gave high scores to pupils who did not deserve them, or that the results were a real muddle. Every year schools sent back copies of the tests so that they could be re-marked, but the government, of whatever complexion, stood by them.

Shakespeare tests

Perhaps the most controversial part of the Sats tests was the Shakespeare test which remained throughout the 14 years. In the first place, some questioned the fact that there was an exam dedicated to Shakespeare at all. While many could see the point of selecting him out for study they could not see why he was privileged in this particular way.

Jane Coles (2004) looked at the way pupils connected the study of his plays with class and notions of Britishness. Writing that, 'The then Conservative Government felt ideologically impelled to impose a sense of shared national heritage' (ibid.) and in particular Shakespeare, she felt that little changed when New Labour came to power, with their talk of 'common values and a perceived need for national identity' and for 'social cohesion and cultural belonging' (ibid.). Shakespeare had been wrapped in a flag and become identified with a very particular view of cultural hegemony. She asked, finally, 'Why, for instance, should all 14 year olds be required to sit national tests at the end of Key Stage 3 in Reading, Writing and Shakespeare' (ibid.)?

Whether one accepted a Shakespeare paper or not, the other major problem was that pupils were getting their first taste of Shakespeare through an examination. While all other exams, both GCSE and A-level, had Shakespeare assessed through coursework, KS3 had an hour and a quarter paper where pupils had to respond to set scenes. There is some evidence that this altered the way Shakespeare was taught (Hodgen and Marshall, 2005). Rather than being taught formatively, with genuine questions about the text at the forefront of teaching, pupils were crammed to be able to answer questions on the areas on which they would be tested, in the play they were studying.

Even the most adventurous of teachers had difficulties avoiding the trap that exams set them. Again Coles (2009) looked at interviews of some pupils studying *Henry V.* The pupils were involved in story boarding, drama and film production, bringing their own interpretations to the text. In particular, at the time, Coles was interested to see how they related to *Henry V* in terms of the war in Iraq, many students having gone on a protest about the conflict. This would seem a very open exploration of the text but she found,

> How strongly the intrusion of explicit SATs preparation (however briefly done at the end of the term's work) had disrupted the students' engagement, causing them to re-conceptualise the play as an exam text. For many of them this had triggered a process of resentful disconnection. (ibid., p. 33)

After looking at more recent examples of Sats teaching, her article concludes 'Even in the hands of an experienced and skilful teacher like Marie, the discourse of the test is likely to intrude in such a way as to close down the classroom' (ibid., p. 47).

Other, more anecdotal evidence suggests the same. In a letter written to the TES, Mike Ferguson claims,

> My students this year engaged again with their Shakespeare text at a time quite deliberately separate from the exam period. We studied the play as it should be studied. Later, a few weeks before their test date, we crammed on the selected scenes they would respond to in the test. This was pure and simple exam preparation which had very little to do with Shakespeare and everything to do with learning the tricks of good exam performance.
>
> There are no rewards to come from the Shakespeare tests. (Ferguson, 13 June 1997)

One of the problems with testing through a timed examination was that Shakespeare became very much a playwright that was studied in text form rather than actively, as had been championed by, among others, Rex Gibson, who in 1986 set up the Shakespeare in Schools project. In March 2008 the Royal Shakespeare Company launched a manifesto called *Stand Up for Shakespeare.* In it the RSC asked schools to 'Do it on your feet See it live Start it earlier'.

This was a call for schools to adopt the active methods as proposed by Gibson, which took Shakespeare off the page and prevented him being prey to close textual analysis. To be fair many of the Sats questions were about how one could dramatize a particular scene but it still required heavy knowledge of the plot and exploration of Bradleyian character and theme. As Ferguson wrote, it still meant cramming the set scenes before the test.

The arguments for a course-based response to Shakespeare was overwhelming in the eyes of many. The chances of actively or dramatically engaging with Shakespeare were seriously diminished because pupils had to be prepared to answer, in written form, whatever an examiner put in front of them. At GCSE, pupils could even have an oral response to Shakespeare; teaching could be far more active as classes could decide what they wanted to respond to in a play of their choice. Keith Davidson, of the National Association for the Teaching of English, claimed,

> We have always argued that teacher assessment is the only way to assess Shakespeare. The questions in the tests are laughable. They are based on a fragment, of a bit, of a passage of a text, and they do nothing to assess a pupil's appreciation. (Davidson, TES, 11 July 2008)

In fact the Shakespeare paper did change in 2002. Up until then pupils received 38 marks for the Shakespeare paper overall – 20 for writing and 18 for reading. In 2002 this changed and a spurious question was introduced that was loosely linked with the play being studied. On the *Macbeth* paper, for example, pupils were asked to write about fictional villains; for *Twelfth Night* about fashion, and for *Henry V* they had to write a motivational speech. The paper as a whole still received 38 marks but now only 18 of them were for studying Shakespeare.

This caused a furore in the press as well as among English teachers. Jane Cole cites one headline in her article of the same name, 'Alas poor Shakespeare' (2003) and Maggie Pitfield (2006) also considers the damage done by assessing Shakespeare in this way and asks again for the assessment of Shakespeare to be rethought. Moreover, although the teachers disliked the fact that Shakespeare was subject to a timed test it was the only piece of literature that was assessed at KS3. To halve the amount of marks the paper was awarded was not only doing down Shakespeare it was dumbing down literature in general.

In 2004, (for the tests to be taken in the summer of 2005) the tests changed again when the short writing task ceased to have anything to do with

Shakespeare at all and was moved to another paper. The Shakespeare paper, however, still only received 18 marks even though exactly the same amount of work had to go into the preparation. English teachers were still far from happy.

The abolition of Sats

Rumors that the Sats were coming to an end began in late 2005 when the government started to pilot what became known as single level tests. They were so called because pupils were to sit them every time their teacher felt that they had arrived at a new level of achievement. The opportunity to take these new tests was to be twice a year and the results were to be just as high-stakes as the previous key stage tests. A bright pupil, for example, might take three tests instead of one at key stage 3 – a level test for levels 5, 6 and 7. They examined comprehension and writing, but not Shakespeare. Although the putative promise of the end of the Sats was tempting, the new single level tests actually meant more examination rather than less and would possibly mean even more interference in the curriculum as pupils would never be free from testing.

In July 2008, the House of Commons Select Committee on Children, Schools and Families, however, reported on the testing arrangements in England. The select committee had, for a number of months, asked those involved in any way with testing their opinions, and research findings, on the assessment regime in England. The report was wide-ranging, but in it the committee found room to criticize the tests as they currently stood. On the purpose of national testing, for example, they wrote:

> We consider that the overemphasis on the importance of national tests, which address only a limited part of the National Curriculum and a limited range of children's skills and knowledge, has resulted in teachers narrowing their focus. (Great Britain Parliament House of Commons Children, Schools and Families Committee, 2008, p. 92)

And again, 'We are concerned about the Government's stance on the merits of the current testing system' (ibid., p. 92). On the consequences of high stakes testing, they wrote: 'We believe that teaching to the test and this inappropriate focus on test results may leave pupils unprepared for higher education and employment' (ibid., p. 94), saying also that they were 'Persuaded by the evidence that it is entirely possible to improve test scores through mechanisms such as teaching to the test, narrowing the curriculum and concentrating effort and resources on borderline students' (p. 94). It was on the single-level tests, however, that they were most emphatic. 'We believe that true personalized learning is incompatible with a high-stakes single level test which focuses on academic learning' (ibid., p. 96). Although those involved in education took note of these findings the government seemed not to heed them.

The final nail in the coffin, in England, for the testing arrangements at key stage 2 and 3 seemingly came somewhat later that summer. For the first time the contract for marking the Sats had gone to ETS (Education and Testing Service), the American company who examine the SATs in the US. The arrangements were a fiasco from start to finish – marking the papers wrongly and failing to assess all the candidates were among the disasters – and eventually their £156m, five-year contract was severed in August 2008.

At the time, the British Government said that it was going to award a single-year contract to a new body. But it seems that even the government realized that this was a mistake. Mary Bousted, the president of the ATL, had called for 'The government . . . to take this golden opportunity to completely overhaul its testing regime, and in the interim should suspend SATs for 2009' (quoted in Lipsett, 2008).

On 14th October, Ed Balls went one stage further and got rid of the KS3 tests altogether, as well as the single-level test in secondary schools and potentially the tests for 11-year-olds. He argued that the main indicator of how a secondary school was doing was the GCSE; that the key stage 3 tests had served their purpose but were no longer necessary and that the single level tests did not differentiate enough between pupils to make them worth pursuing. At KS2, however, his sentiments were somewhat different. He said that the tests were 'essential to giving parents, teachers and the public the information they need about the progress of every primary age child and every primary school' (Balls, 2008). They were to continue to evaluate the single-level tests.

The expert group on assessment

As part of his announcement Ed Balls set up a group on assessment. Originally due to report in February 2009 they finally produced the report in May. For 11- to 14-year-olds (KS3) English they recommended two things. The first was an Assessment Performance Unit (APU) type arrangement where approximately 10,000, 14-year-olds would be assessed to establish a database on national performance. Individuals would not receive scores nor would schools. The test results would just be fed into a database for national accountability.

The government has asked that, TIMMS style (the international maths tests), we cooperate with other English speaking countries on a literacy test (DCSF, 2009, p. 32–5.) The difficulty with this test is that it may involve multiple-choice questions which demand a 'right' answer.

The other major recommendation made by the expert group was the establishment of APP This was because they took for granted that APP was a part of Assessment for Learning (AfL). They stated that the 'DCSF and its partners should continue to promote Assessment for Learning, including the use of Assessing Pupils' Progress materials, in all primary and secondary schools through the existing strategy' because it 'has improved the quality of [teachers'] assessments'. It concludes that, 'done well, APP . . . could have a very positive impact on the quality of teaching and learning' (DCSF 2009, pp. 11–13).

Assessing pupils' profile

We will deal with APP in more specific detail later on in Chapter 6 but for now it is worth noting how it came about. It was originally called Monitoring Pupils' Progress and was introduced in pilot form in September 2003. The project initially involved 77 schools in 13 local authorities. Of these schools, 40 continued into the second year of the project and were joined by 29 other schools from a variety of authorities. Initially MPP was introduced solely for English at KS3 to find, among other things, if, 'agreement between teachers and markers could be investigated' (QCA, 2006 p. 17) and 'whether they would provide a reliable measure of progress within the key stage' (ibid., p. 17). This they explored along with the optional tests, which had been introduced for Years 7 and 8.

No such agreement was found. There was little overlap between the levels awarded by teachers and the markers of the Sats. In the first year it was carried out there was 61 per cent for reading and 70 per cent for writing. At the end of the second year it was even worse with only 56 per cent for reading and 59 per cent for writing (ibid., pp. 39–40). The optional tests were lower still (ibid., 37–8).

Moreover, it appears that despite much talk of the formative nature of the MPP, they were used entirely summatively.

> MPP assessments are unique in offering outcomes that are diagnostic, giving precise and detailed information about strengths and weaknesses in relation to specific AFs and, at the same time, providing a summative level judgement. (ibid., p. 4)

However, 'There was also some evidence that in the case of some pupils, MPP had showed they were capable of more than teachers has realized or had expected of them' (ibid., p. 51) but the ratification of this as with all of the work done on MPP seems to have been done by QCA alone. Although the report claims that, 'Every stage of the project was the subject of independent evaluation' (ibid., p. 10), no other body is mentioned as having completed it.

In 2006 MPP was renamed APP or assessing, rather than monitoring pupil progress as if the name had a better feel. The monitoring of pupils sounds slightly more officious and official than simply assessing them but the basis for that monitoring or assessment was almost identical. As with MPP progress was linked to a number of Assessment Foci more of which will be discussed in Chapter 6. The major difference was that these AFs were now for each level including levels 1, 2, 7 and 8, and the QCA-provided tasks no longer had to be used. Again it was initially for English only but a year later maths and science were included and it was extended into the primary sector.

By 2008 the Government had committed itself to spending £150 million over three years with the aim of ensuring that all schools will have embedded APP as part of their assessment process by 2011, including foundation subjects (DCSF, 2008). Laurie Smith explores that justification of this in an article (2009) where he finds no external or research rationale for expanding the APP programme. He looks in particular at the way APP has been linked to AfL and finds very little overlap if any at all.

He writes:

> The Assessment for Learning Strategy, the DCSF policy statement emphasises APP throughout and makes little reference to AfL. For example, 'The benefits of assessment for learning' occupies a half-page and consists chiefly of nine of the Assessment Reform Group's 10 Principles (ARG, 2002) presented in jigsaw format (the omitted principle is 'has an emotional impact'). But this is followed by a half-page listing six aspects and purposes of assessment described in functional terms. . . For example, 'accurate assessment' is defined as 'knowing what the standards are, judging pupils' work correctly and making accurate assessments linked to the National Curriculum' (DCSF, 2008, p. 5). Assessment is therefore deemed to be accurate only if it judges pupils' work in relation to the National Curriculum. Other kinds of formative assessment, as described by Black and William and others, are excluded. (Smith, 2009)

What is clear, however, from the expert panel's report is that APP, for the moment, is their idea of the future of KS3 assessment.

Wales

The situation in Wales is somewhat different. The National curriculum arrived at the same time in Wales as it did in England though even then it looked slightly different. Wales had to have a different curriculum from England because a large number of the student population were educated through the medium of Welsh and therefore English was a second language. When the new curriculum came in in 1995, unlike England, Wales did not have a fixed canon to follow. The Sats, however, remained. But in 1999 Wales achieved a degree of independence from Westminster, and in 2001 it published a document called *The Learning Country*. This was followed by the abolition of Sats for 7-year-olds and in 2003 by the Assessment Review Group which undertook a study of the testing arrangements for the rest of the pupils in its schools. Professor Richard Daugherty was placed in charge of the group, which reported in 2004. Although he too only had a brief period of time to produce the report, he had longer than his Westminster friends.

In an interview about the recommendations of *Learning pathways through statutory assessment: Key Stages 2 and 3*, he concluded:

> What the Group has tried to do, by reviewing all the evidence we could find and taking the best available advice, is to learn from the experience of the past ten years. We have concluded that some features of the current arrangements, such as assessment by teachers at the end of each key stage, should be retained but strengthened. Other features, such as the core subject tests taken at the same time as teachers are making their assessments, should be phased out. (Daugherty, 2004a)

Again the tests were to be replaced by an APU style assessment for 15-year-olds, so that international comparisons might be made, and skills tests were to be introduced for the penultimate year of primary schools. Work in the final year of primary school was to be moderated by teachers in primary and secondary schools in the same education authority. KS3 pupils were to be assessed by coursework. The group also recommended 'The development of assessment for learning practices should be a central feature of a programme of development in Wales of curriculum and assessment' (Daugherty, 2004b, p. 31).

The arrangements for the assessment of KS3 pupils have now been going for two years. Not all schools have to submit their work for external moderation every year but a sample do and the requirements are not unlike those for the NEAB.

The aim of the 'external moderation' is 'to support and strengthen subject departments' systems and procedures for internal standardization of teacher assessment' (WJEC, CBAC, 2008, p. 3). What is more, 'The sample evidence for external moderation should reflect the broad range of contexts and types of activity/outcomes that characterize normal classwork and out of class activities' (ibid., p. 3). In other words it is attempting to capture all that is done at KS3 not just a small part of it. In order to do this they suggest that six pieces of work are assessed – two from each attainment target – each showing slightly different attributes.

In Speaking and Listening, which they have significantly renamed 'Oracy' they have to have evidence of group work and either a role-play or an 'individual talk'. The combining of the two components, speaking and listening, into one word 'oracy' is significant in that, in some ways, it reinforces that both are equally important. It also references a study, The National Oracy Project, chaired by John Johnson, that started work in 1986 and was finally published in 1993. This was designed to revolutionize talk in the classroom and put a great deal of weight on classroom dialogue as a method of learning. The first piece of work that they have to show – group work – is evidence of the importance of the project. The second, however, is somewhat confusing. There is a great deal of difference between a talk and role-play. Apart from anything else, one would presumably demonstrate the ability to listen, the other not.

The one for reading asks that they should have two pieces of work – one should a literary text and the other non-literary. The literary piece does not, significantly, have to be on a whole book; the non-literary, which can include media, should have 'a significant amount of "language" for exploration by pupils' (WJEC, CBAC, 2008, p. 9). Reading is to be assessed entirely through the writing but at no point do they suggest that one might assess the writing in a reading assignment, or assess reading through oracy. Of the writing tasks – one should be personal or imaginative, the other 'transactional' (ibid., p. 10). Again the word transactional is an interesting choice as it avoids the 2005 National Curriculum writing triplets, for example persuasive writing, which became so embedded in English teaching in England.

When being moderated, English departments are asked to collect evidence, which shows a range of abilities in the classroom and shows 'a *collective* understanding and application of national curriculum standards for each attainment target' (ibid., p. 3, emphasis is the original). The word collective is interesting as it shows the need for a joint, or departmental understanding not just that of an individual or head of department. It emphasizes the need for a community of interpreters deciding what the national curriculum levels might be. It must also be clear in the individual teacher's work.

> *In order for the sample evidence to be moderated effectively the accompanying teacher commentaries will need to be sufficiently detailed to convey the subject department's understanding of standards to the external moderators.*
>
> The teacher commentaries should provide the rationale that underpins the subject department's collective understanding of the standard of the pupils' work selected. (ibid., p. 4 emphasis in the original)

Teachers then, show a departmental view rather than an individual perspective, and even more interesting 'the rationale' or reasoning behind 'the subject department's collective understanding of the standard of the pupils' work selected'. This cannot be arbitrary. It must 'underpin' the decision. Each piece of work, therefore, must act almost as an exemplar of the department's choice. The problem is that that commentaries have to be 'sufficiently detailed'. This may mean that the texts themselves, for example, will have to be annotated, indicating what it is that the pupil has said that means it is, say, a level 5. This is further reinforced when they add, 'When cross referencing teachers' commentaries to the pupils' work, the precise location of evidence within pupils' work should be pinpointed by highlighting, labelling and/or annotation' (ibid., p. 6). This means either a post hoc rationalization of a pupils piece of work or specific teaching to the level descriptors, which may detract from viewing a piece of work holistically.

At the point of writing this there is insufficient evidence to tell how the work is going in Wales and whether or not they are marking the portfolios of work holistically or atomistically; whether they are teaching to the part, or to the whole. There is little to tell also about the moderation procedures in general and to what extent they are working in terms of the reliability of assessment.

Scotland

Scotland has always had a system of education that differs slightly from its nearest neighbours and the retention of a national assessment of pupils as a whole, the Assessment of Achievement Programme, was one way in which they established that difference. 5 per cent of pupils at 8, 11 and 13 were monitored in reading, writing and maths. In 2004 this was replaced by the Scottish Survey of Achievement, and social studies was added into the programme. Pupils are now assessed every four years. This meant that the Scots already felt that some kind of national survey of standards was happening.

This may have had an impact when another major reform was taking place south of the border. As England and Wales introduced a statutory national curriculum, with mandatory testing at 7, 11, and 14, Scotland introduced non-statutory National Guidelines. These were phased in during the 1990s, the Scottish Office having passed the *Curriculum and Assessment in Scotland: A policy for the 1990s* in 1987.

The National Guidelines in themselves are interesting in that they are slightly different from their English equivalents. They, too, have attainment targets but instead of the first one being called Speaking and Listening it is called Listening and the second is called Talking. It may mean nothing but it is interesting that they have put listening first, implying its significance, and that it is followed by the word 'talk'. 'Talk', in some ways, has a more dialogic feel to it. If you speak it can mean that you speak alone. You have, for example speakers at conferences or debates; you have keynote speakers. Here the person has, in effect, become the verb; the person has become the speaker. You can give a talk, but then the person who is giving the talk is separated out from the verb. There is the idea of a talker but seen in that context the idea of a talker has a somewhat pejorative feel. It is a person who talks too much. Talking is also more ordinary, every day. Speaking is somehow a more delicate or refined word.

The attainment targets are split up into strands. These too are significant. Reading, for example has three strands Reading for Pleasure, Reading for Information and Reading to Appreciate the Writer's Craft. To begin with it divides up what we mean by reading, putting first, and, therefore, possibly most importantly reading for pleasure. After the Cox curriculum, reading for pleasure was given virtually no prominence at all and even then it was not singled out as a separate strand. Presumably it was very difficult to assess how much someone was reading for the sheer enjoyment of reading.

Significantly they separate this out from reading for 'information' and reading to 'appreciate the writer's craft'. One way of understanding this is that reading to be informed is not a pleasant activity just one that has to be done. It is also different from appreciation. Appreciation is an interesting choice of words as well. Again it is more associated with liking, and also in some ways, connoisseurship, than, for example, the word criticism. What they are being asked to 'appreciate' is the 'craft of a writer'. The word craft connotes both the artistry and artisanship of the writer.

Although it was mooted that there should be compulsory tests, as there were in England and Wales, after much public debate and disquiet, it was agreed that while they were mandatory, pupils should do tests as and when they were ready. Having said, however, that the curriculum was only a guideline and that the tests could be done as and when a pupil needed it, most schools followed the National Guidelines (Daugherty and Ecclestone, 2009) This was partly because Her Majesty's Inspectors of Education (HMIE) used them as the core of their inspection process. And the tests began to dominate. As Louise Hayward, wrote,

> Attainment targets dominated thinking in schools and classrooms and National Tests were used to decide whether or not a child had achieved a level of attainment in English and mathematics. Rather than being used to confirm or to challenge teachers' professional judgement, National Tests were replacing it. (2007, p. 255)

Again, in language that has become all too familiar, testing becomes synonymous with measuring a child's attainment rather than the totality of what they might achieve.

> A single test can only sample a very small part of the content of a programme or course and so may not give the student a chance to show what s/he knows and can do . . . 'Ability' comes to be defined as what is measured in tests, rather than as learning what is taught in programmes and, because the score or grade looks seductively tidy and exact, we attribute considerably more meaning to it than is actually justified by the evidence. (Hutchinson and Hayward, 2005, p. 242)

Possibly for these reasons, the now Scottish Assembly debated the role of assessment in Scotland. Jack McConnell, who was at the time in charge of education but later became First Minister, 'Argued that assessment should be designed to improve learning and achievement' and that they 'Needed a coherent and effective system of assessment that was clearly focused on promoting progress and learning' (ibid., p. 232). As a result he formed the Assessment Action Group, which was to oversee research being carried out on the 3–14 age group. This became known as Assessment is for Learning (AifL).

As Hutchinson and Hayward argue, 'The programme's title asserted the view of the wider educational community that the main purpose of assessment should be to support learning' (ibid., p. 232). It also showed that the movement had political support.

As a result a consultation on the whole assessment system was set up, including all the major stakeholders in education such as teachers, parents and universities, as well as policy makers like the Scottish Qualifications Authority (SQA). When they reported, they had decided that they wanted a manageable change to take place but not a 'revolutionary' one, and they wanted 'Assessment not measurement' to be the 'key concern' (ibid., p. 233).

Crucial to the tentative success of the programme was that they attempted to integrate all Scotland's methods of assessments and subtly but radically transform them. They had been commissioned to look at three things: how to make assessment for learning a reality in classrooms; how to reconcile this with assessment for accountability and, lastly, how to stop the whole assessment process being the bureaucratic nightmare it was fast becoming and to focus instead upon what pupils learned.

The biggest change came about with Assessment is for Learning, which looked at the work being done in this area. They drew heavily on the research of Black and Wiliam (1998a, 1998b) and also the Kings Medway Oxfordshire Formative Assessment Project (KMOFAP (2003)). We will look at KMOFAP in more detail in the next chapter, but the Scottish team, included as consultants, many of the researchers and teachers, who were involved in KMOFAP. By 2007, there was a limited confidence that it was going in the right direction. A report was carried out on how the consultation process with King's, among others, had gone. Hallam et al. (2004) were positive. They reported that there were 'relatively few difficulties in implementation'; a 'dramatic improvement in pupils' learning skills' and 'a shift away from teacher-centred pedagogy'.

But, as was said before, what the team was attempting to do was to integrate all aspects of assessment. Hayward in 2007 identifies what she means by an AiFL school.

> An AifL school is described as one which actively and coherently promotes Assessment for Learning (assessment action by teachers to help pupil's learning); Assessment as Learning (involvement of pupils in self-and peer-assessment and in personal learning planning through discussion with their teachers); and Assessment of Learning (accurate and moderated summative assessment of standards of performance). (Hayward, 2007, p. 261)

This is very different from what she had written with Hutchinson two years earlier. Talking about the limitations of the previous system she wrote,

> If the data about student attainment at individual level are based on such limited evidence and are therefore less than dependable as representations of learning, the aggregate will likewise be a limited basis for making important judgements about a school's effectiveness in promoting learning. Just as using test scores alone is unlikely to represent the complexity of a student's learning and may adversely affect the student's attitude and motivation to learn, so evidence about a school's performance limited to aggregated attainment data is unlikely to provide a full picture of the effectiveness of a complex organization. It may adversely affect the staff's motivation to improve its provision or it may distort classroom practice, as teachers strive to improve their position in a rank order of attainment results, rather than take steps to improve the overall quality of students' learning. (Hutchinson and Hayward, 2005, p. 242)

Two years on and she is able to write,

> AifL has made a difference to assessment 3–14 in Scotland. It has influenced teachers' classroom practices, schools' assessment policies and the ways in which national and local policy-makers interact with schools and with one another. The nature of that difference is only beginning to emerge. (Hayward, 2007, p. 261)

Assessment is for learning, then has become a central focus in the Scottish system and it is the clearest in its commitment to AfL in the UK.

Conclusion

The situation differs, therefore, almost radically between the three countries of Great Britain. The situation in Northern Ireland is different again, because it has had, until very recently, selection at 11. What is interesting is that in a climate where, in England at least, everything became so centralized and government controlled, AfL, or class-based, formative assessment, became so prominent. Admittedly this is less so in Wales, and in particular Scotland, where the formative and summative, in some respects, worked together collaboratively, but in England AfL was the only part of helping children to learn that teachers could be said to have some say in given the plethora of tests and exams children are expected to take. In the next chapter, therefore, we will look at the influence of AfL in England, focusing in particular, at KMOFAP.

4 Assessment for learning and KMOFAP

Formative assessment became voguish in 1998 with the publication of Paul Black and Dylan Wiliam's article, called 'Assessment and Classroom Learning' (1998a) which was sponsored by the Assessment Reform Group. This was followed by *Inside the Black Box* (1998b), which put the findings into a more readable, user friendly form. But the term had been around for far longer. Two books, for example, which had been investigating formative practice in the primary classroom had come out, in the case of one book five years earlier, and another came out at around the same time as Black and Wiliam's. Torrance and Pryor's book, *Investigating Formative Assessment: Teaching, learning and assessment in the classroom* (1998) was published in the same year but was based on a research project that predated publication, and Mary Jane Drummond's book, *Assessing Children's Learning,* was first published in 1993.

Both these books, while talking of the huge benefits of formative assessment, acknowledged that it was quite difficult to do. Black and Wiliam's article and subsequent pamphlet, however, made formative assessment much more achievable but even they added,

> Teachers will not take up attractive sounding ideas, albeit based on extensive research, if these are presented as general principles, which leave entirely to them the task of translating them into everyday practice. (Black and Wiliam, 1998b, p. 15)

Their research, on which the findings were based, were indeed 'attractive' and 'extensive'. Having looked at over 250 articles they found that when formative assessment was applied, pupils could increase their performance by between 0.4 and 0.7 of a grade. That is the equivalent of increasing our performance in maths, for example, from somewhere in the middle ranking of the international tables to near the top. It was, however, merely an academic exercise if teachers did not take on board the findings because they were left with 'translating them into everyday practice'.

For this reason Black and Wiliam embarked on the King's Medway Oxfordshire Formative Assessment Project (KMOFAP) to try to see how these general principles, as they then saw them, of formative practice could be put to use by teachers. It was a three-year project in which they worked closely with the two local authorities involved. They started with the following strategies, derived from the research, in an attempt to make the findings seem less theoretical: classroom questioning; sharing success criteria with learner; feedback with the learner; peer and self-assessment and the formative use of summative tests. Each of these was discussed and practised, initially by maths and science teachers and then, 18 months later, by English teachers. A book was later published on the project called *Assessment for Learning: Putting it into practice* (2003). We will discuss the work that was done with English teachers later on in the chapter.

The research was taken up in a major way by government agencies, such as Ofsted, and, too, the then DfES. From 2003 to 2007 the DfES' site proliferated with information about approaches to AfL. A version of it was adopted as part of the government's KS3 strategy and a pamphlet introducing AfL was brought out in 2003, providing 'a description of the principles underpinning effective practice, practical examples and suggestions for trying things out in the classroom' (DfES, 2003). In 2004 the literacy strategies came on board and towards the end of that year a study unit on AfL was published in the Pedagogy and Practice series (DfES, 2004b).

In 2007 *The Assessment for Learning 8 schools project* (DfES, 2007) was in theory a look at how at how certain schools, including several English departments, implemented AfL in their classrooms. Lessons were videoed and different teams looked at how the schools had gone about implementing feedback to pupils, questioning and peer assessment. The aim of the project was,

> To identify what helps pupils develop as motivated and effective learners and how AfL can be successfully developed whole school through professional dialogue and collaborative working with teachers, school leaders and local authorities. (ibid., p. 6)

Versions of AfL found their way into the personalized learning agenda and this, too, came out of the DfES. David Hargreaves, who was for a time the chair of the QCA, described assessment for learning as 'a teaching strategy of very high leverage' (2004, p. 24) and, out of his concern for AfL, came personalized learning. He influenced both the think tank Demos and David Miliband, then Schools Standards Minister, who wrote a pamphlet for the Specialist Schools Trust called *Personalised Learning: A Route to Excellence and Equity* (2003). The idea was that through AfL one would get the personalization of learning required.

All this meant that AfL was placed firmly on the political and so the schools' agenda. In the vast majority of high schools now, there is usually someone, within the school, held responsible for assessment both formative and summative. When, in 2008, the government set up an Expert Group on Assessment, apart from recommending an end to the Sats for 14-year-olds, the group advised that each school should have a chartered assessor. They also recommended that the DCSF should work with other assessment organizations, such as exam boards, to develop a national scheme of accreditation of schools with a mark of excellence at assessment (DCSF, 2009).

This coincides with the DCSF's *Assessment for Learning Strategy* (2008), which recommended having a senior assessment specialist in every school. It echoes, too, the idea proposed by the Chartered Institute of Educational Assessors who also wish to see at least one chartered assessor in every school. Their aim, as a charitable organization, is 'to improve the quality of assessment in schools and colleges by working with educational assessors to develop their knowledge, understanding and capability in all aspects of educational testing and assessment' (http://www.ciea.org.uk).

Forms of Assessment for Learning

The difficulty with formative assessment, however, was that although the idea had become very popular with institutions such as the DCSF and other policy making institutions, it was quite hard to achieve. Mary James in a conference speech made the following observation about how AfL had been applied.

> Assessment for learning' is becoming a catch-all phrase, used to refer to a range of practices. In some versions it has been turned into a series of ritualised procedures. In others it is taken to be more concerned with monitoring and recording than with using information to help learning. (James, 2004, p. 2)

Earlier advocates, such as Drummond or Torrance and Prior, might also have suggested that the kind of practices proposed by these organizations might not have been the assessment for learning that they recognized. The DCSF version was, for example very target driven and Mary-Jane Drummond argues against a model of assessment of 'checklists, precision, explicit criteria [and] incontrovertible facts and figures'. Rather she is arguing for a method that can 'describe the ways in which, in our everyday practice, we observe children's learning, strive to understand it, and then put our understanding to good use' (2003, p. 13). This view of assessment leads her to eschew the model of assessment in which 'the assessor collects the evidence, makes judgements on the basis of that evidence, and then certain events follow' (ibid., p. 14). Instead she sees the process as 'essentially provisional, partial, tentative, exploratory and, inevitably, incomplete' (ibid., p. 14). The work of Torrance and Pryor discussed the possibility of early years teachers approaching assessment for learning in a very similar way, distinguishing between 'divergent' as opposed to 'convergent' formative assessment (1998) and this, too, opposes the methods as set out in various DCSF documents.

Much of the early work on AfL had actually been done by maths and science teachers rather than English teachers. Mary James looks at some of the reasons why this might be in her chapter on 'Assessment Teaching and Theories of Learning', in the book *Assessment and Learning* (2009). Looking at the three dominant theories that have researched into assessment – behaviourism, cognitive constructivism and social constructivism – she writes that the one that has achieved most attention until recently is cognitive constructivism and this is linked most closely to science and maths education.

Although, she writes, it is not easy to define because 'cognitive theories are complex',

> In essence, the role of the teacher is to help 'novices' to acquire 'expert' understanding of conceptual structures and processing strategies to solve problems with symbolic manipulation with 'less search'. In view of the importance of prior learning as an influence on new learning, formative assessment emerges as an important integral element of pedagogic practice because it is necessary to elicit students' mental models. (James, 2009, p. 55)

In some respects this fits very nicely with the work that Paul Black and Dylan Wiliam did initially in KMOFAP, beginning as it did with maths and science teachers. Students' prior learning was emphasized and so was the gap between this learning and what they were about to learn. In fact they made great emphasis on the gap in pupil learning. As we have seen, the idea of a 'gap' in learning comes from Royce Sadler (1989). Black and Wiliam, rather like the cognitive constructivists, appeared to think of gap as something definable. A teacher needs to have knowledge of a pupil's prior learning in order to construct a model of what they need to learn next, in other words how to fill the gap. But Sadler's work is more ambiguous. To quote him once again,

> The greater the divergence in outcomes which can be regarded as acceptable, the more likely it is that a variety of ways can be devised to alter the gap between actual and reference levels, and therefore the less likely it is that information about the gap will in itself suggest a remedial action. (Sadler, 1989, p. 139)

In other words knowing their prior knowledge does not necessarily give you information on what they need to do next in order to fill the gap. But the questioning techniques that Black and Wiliam introduced were about teasing out pupil misconceptions about what they were learning in order that these could be identified and then rectified.

Eighteen months into the project, however, English teachers joined. English teachers have not had the same history of formative assessment for a variety of reasons. To begin with they do not have a strong cognitive constructivist view of their subject, particularly if they take an arts view of English. English does not progress in a tidy, definable way. There are no misconceptions that need to be rectified before a pupil can go forward. It is a much messier affair.

The other is that if English teachers have any philosophy at all, particularly those who take an arts view of the subject, it is to the work of Lev Vygotsky. Vygotsky, as most English teachers understand him, believed that children learned through the language they used, that language was an essential cognitive tool. James Britton, among others, rediscovered the Russian psychologist in the 1960s, writing books such as *Language and Learning*,(1974) and, with Douglas Barnes and Harold Rosen, *Language, the Learner and the School*, (1972). In particular Britton and others believed that Vygotsky's theory of the Zone of Proximal Development (ZPD) was especially relevant to how children learned. Vygotsky defined the ZPD as,

> the distance between the actual development level as determined by individual problem solving and the level of potential as determined through problem solving under adult guidance or in collaboration with more capable peers. (Vygotsky, 1978, p. 86)

In other words children improved by talking and discussing with people who were slightly better than themselves at whatever was being talked or discussed. Each new activity on which a child embarked produced another ZPD. Vygotsky's thinking was taken up by Bruner, who promoted a model of 'social interaction, negotiation and shared learning' (Bruner cited in Corden, 2000, p. 9). Like Vygotsky he concludes that 'most learning in most settings is a communal activity' (ibid., p. 9).

This concept of social learning is essential to a socially constructed view of learning. As Mary James writes in this model of assessment,

> Thinking is conducted through actions that alter the situation and the situation changes the thinking; the two constantly interact . . . Since language, which is central to our capacity to think, is developed in relationship between people, social relationships are necessary for, and precede, learning (Vygotsky, 1978). Thus learning is by definition a social and collaborative activity in which people develop their thinking together. (James, 2009, p. 57)

So 'Teachers and students jointly solve problems and all develop their skill and understanding' (ibid., p. 57). This is because,

> It is important to find activities that learners can complete with assistance but not alone so that 'the more expert other', in some cases the teacher but often a peer, can 'scaffold' their learning (a concept shared with cognitive approaches) and remove the scaffold when they can cope on their own. (ibid., p. 57)

Using this socio-cultural approach James writes, 'The teacher needs to create an environment in which people can be stimulated to think and act' (ibid., p. 57). Roy Cordon, in his book on language in the primary classroom, talks of Bruner's interpretation of Vygotsky. He says that for Bruner, 'learning is facilitated through the provision of organized and structured learning experiences and opportunities for children to extend their current understandings' (Corden, 2000, pp. 8–9). This is the scaffolding Mary James speaks of. Bruner then goes on to argue that speech is an essential part of this process because it enables pupils to make sense of new ideas and concepts and through this process progression takes place.

English involvement with KMOFAP

In their later work Paul Black and Dylan Wiliam have made it much clearer that they actually support a socially constructivist view of assessment rather than a cognitive one (see Black and Wiliam, 2009). It is evident, too, that the English teachers involved in KMOFAP seemed to sympathize, either knowingly or implicitly, with this position. For this reason it is worth examining the role that English teachers played in the project, by examining the interviews that they gave.

As has already been said the English teachers arrived 18 months into the project. They were included because it was felt that it was important to have all three of the core subjects within the project. Why they were not included from the beginning is not altogether clear but the maths and science teachers felt that they had started earlier because they were the 'remedial' group, English teachers being so far ahead of them. Whether or not their perception is true it has to be said that the four meetings that were carried out in college had a very different feel from the ones held jointly for maths and science. Peer assessment, which we shall talk about later, was, for example, practised, in some form or other, by all the English teachers involved, in a way that it had not been for maths and science.

Each teacher was also visited twice during the course of the project both to be seen teaching and to be interviewed. All of the teachers who were initially involved in the project were interviewed both in general, about the terms of the project, and, too, about the specific lesson which had been observed and it is these interviews that we will initially look at. To begin with they were read in terms of critical appraisal (Eisner, 2005) and this was important. Elliot Eisner has written at length on the importance of educational research taking an arts as well as a science approach to the research process. In particular he talks about criticism and connoisseurship. While acknowledging that some may view criticism as being 'subjective' he argues, 'Each of these concepts, educational connoisseurship and educational criticism, have their roots in the arts' (ibid., p. 41). He goes on to say,

> Criticism, as Dewey pointed out in *Art as Experience*, has at its end the re-education of perception. What the critic strives for is to articulate or render those ineffable qualities constituting art in the language that makes them vivid. (ibid., p. 41)

And he concludes, 'The task of the critic is to help us see' (ibid., p. 41). If part of the brief of this book is to see English as an arts subject, then it is important to use some of those skills in English in the task of analysing interviews – practical criticism. Part also of practical criticism is assessing what is said. Thus the art of criticism then becomes twofold – it is both an arts discipline and it is about assessment – assessing texts. Whether, as Eisner has it, it helps us see an issue with more clarity than before, is in part, of the job of the critic, but it also lies with the reader as to whether or not they agree with the criticisms, or points of view, made.

The interviews

English as a subject

Perhaps the most surprising feature of the interviews was that for some of the teachers it was a chance to talk about the nature of the subject as it related to formative assessment. Daniel and Kate discuss what it means to motivate children in English and whether this has anything to do with what the subject particularly constitutes. In both the lessons I had observed that the pupils were highly engaged. I was interested, however, in whether or not the pupils had a clear idea of what they were doing in 'English', whether or not they were conceptualizing at any point whether this made them good at English. One was teaching persuasive writing through travel brochures and the other was looking at the history of English, in this instance, by looking at Elizabethan swearing. Daniel, who does most of the speaking, had taught on the history of English, answered,

> That's a really interesting question. And sometimes you can tell how much understanding there is by how much they are engaged because if they are not understanding it they can't be engaged in some circumstances. There are other

> times when they can be, you know, merrily sticking bits of paper to other bits of paper and it could be, you know, a beautiful montage photo collection of the exciting world of Kenya, for your travel brochure . . . You grin and say that's lovely to an extent. (Daniel)

In other words at certain points it is difficult to tell. Understanding, motivation and engagement might be interrelated but they might not. Someone who seems to understand what they are doing may just be happy sticking on bits of paper and have no idea why they are doing, for instance, travel brochures in English. The fact that they are engaged in a piece of persuasive writing, which in itself is part of what you are trying to achieve in English, may have passed them by. Earlier, when talking about his own scheme of work, Daniel says,

> It's not about learning to speak or write in a different language. It's about how language has changed, and hopefully, I think, in a kind of . . . on your differentiated, some will be able to, a few may be able to . . . it's a question of recognising that language has changed and some will recognise how language has changed, what influence, and hopefully most of them will see what has influenced language. (Daniel)

What is interesting is that he repeats what the scheme is about four times 'it's about how language has changed', 'recognising that language has changed', 'recognise how language has changed' and 'what has influenced language' each time varying, just slightly what the scheme is about. At first it is 'about' the very fact that language changes and nothing else; then it becomes 'recognising' it. Recognition is more than simply being 'about' something, it is acknowledging it and, in acknowledging it, some but not all will 'recognise how language has changed'. The 'how' here is important. You may recognize change but not be aware of 'how' it has changed and this brings in the last point, which he mentions – that language is 'influenced'. There are influences in society that can bring about change. Throughout he constantly refines what he thinks. His slightly hesitant, often circuitous, manner suggests that he is thinking through, or even musing upon, the scheme in relation to some overall, larger concept of language – how it is perceived and conceived. Immediately afterwards, however, he reverts to the practicalities of the scheme, what the pupils will actually do.

> Yeah that's basically what we're doing. We've looked at . . . we've talked about, you know, words and that, words that have died and we've talked about Anglo Saxons and invaders and Chaucer. And then we'll move on to more recent

> influences, computers, inventions, slang and then onto accent and dialect and then at the end of term they will do a leaflet on English as was and English as it is. (Daniel)

And this in part is one of the difficulties of English. At what point do pupils understand why they are completing an activity rather than being simply engaged in what they are doing and, if they are not engaged, in the why how do they progress in English? How do they get better if the greater aim, the concept of English, is not made plain? This is something which Daniel grapples with later on in the interview.

> Clearly they were fantastically engaged but the conceptual level, how do you, you know, how do you tease those things out and what are you actually wanting them to learn? Do you know what I mean? And does that make us dull people if we are asking those kind of questions? (Daniel)

Although the last statement was possibly made partly in jest there is a serious point to it. He is concerned about what his pupils are learning yet this has to be teased out. For Peter, in some respects, the point of teaching English is even vaguer but he seems to have come to terms with it in a way that Daniel, perhaps, has not, or rather has not learned how to articulate the point. Peter talks of his teaching and comments at one point,

> I don't think I've ever taught anybody anything. I have a strong feeling that I've never actually done that. People have learned stuff but you know, how they've done that is the really interesting thing. And they you know it has to be true that if you give them time to think . . . that's got to encourage them in the idea that a process of thought can lead somewhere. So that they're not engaged in this kind of guerilla activity, where they are just picking up stuff here and there on a rather sporadic level. But that there is something called a natural rhythm of thought and a process of thought, which you know is a kind of internal dialogue. (Peter)

Although he discusses a great deal of what goes on in his lessons, in a way that is not what is important; it is incidental. What he is attempting to create is a space in which pupils can think. To this extent he echoes what Mary James has to say about socially constructed learning where, 'The teacher needs to create an environment in which people can be stimulated to think and act' (James, 2009, p. 57). He believes that all he can do is give them 'the idea that a process of thought can lead somewhere'. His vehicle for doing so is literature.

In some respects his sentiments echo those of Medway. Medway, in attempting to answer the question of how English can remain in an arts paradigm but still be culturally analytic, has talked about the importance of knowing how rather than knowing about (Medway, 2003a). While acknowledging, almost celebrating the idea that English is, at one level, 'about life' he concludes, 'What you come out of an English course with is not or the important part is not – knowledge you can write out in a test' (Medway, 2003b, p. 5). And for Peter 'they're not engaged in this kind of guerilla activity, where they are just picking up stuff here and there on a rather sporadic level' (Peter), which they then reproduce in exams.

Questioning, oral feedback and dialogue

This links with the way in which both questioning and feedback can be viewed, in as much as they are related to subject knowledge. The issue of subject knowledge, as we have seen, can be highly problematic. If English is viewed as a technical or communication skill then the nature of subject knowledge is fairly straightforward. There are facts, which need to be acquired, which are either right or wrong. Questioning becomes a means by which you determine whether or not a child has learned them. This is the kind of knowledge that Medway believes 'you can write out in a test'. But if one takes a more arts view of the English curriculum, as Medway suggests, where one accumulates knowledge in an almost arbitrary fashion, and there is no designated path of progress, then questioning becomes more difficult on the one hand and yet potentially much more rewarding. This is because it can lead to a genuine dialogue with the pupil where there is no correct answer. The teacher is simply finding out what the pupils think and expanding upon that.

For the KMOFAP teacher, Peter, in some ways, the technisist view of English is 'picking up stuff here and there on a sporadic level'. And this he views as a 'guerilla activity'. Much of what he does, by contrast, seems to be at an instinctive level. Whether this is properly formative assessment is a moot point but his actions seem to be a response to the class he is teaching. He introduces the notion of questioning when talking about reading to a class and even this seems about his own rapport with the pupils.

> The shape of the lesson. I am always conscious not to do things for too long. Occasionally I will read for twenty minutes but that will be determined by whether the group's tolerating that amount of time. So my antennae is out all the time in terms of what's the mood of the group. (Peter)

What he relies on then is his own sense of whether or not a group is responding to his stimulus, whether they are 'tolerating' it. The only mechanism, which is a kind of feedback, is his 'antennae'. I found, in observing his lessons twice, that he seemed to know instinctively when to stop and when to move on. On those occasions when he did not get it right he would acknowledge it. What is interesting is what he does to break the flow of reading. He asks questions. 'If I think things are not, you know, their concentration is going, then I stop and just ask questions about what we've read and then read on' (Peter).

This is very different from the way Black and Wiliam conceived of questioning. Questioning was a way of establishing a pupil's misconceptions of a particular issue. In the book *Assessment for Learning* there is a whole chapter on the way in which you formulate questions, the way you pre-plan them. Peter's technique seems more ad hoc and ad libbed, asking questions when the pupils appear to have lost concentration. He asks the class questions, 'Partly just to check that the plot is being followed, anything about what's revealed about character, what's revealed about ideas in the book, and to give them a break from either my voice or whoever is reading' (ibid.). He concludes, 'So it's, I think it's all about, you know, it's variety really' (ibid.). Questioning, then, becomes about the over all 'shape of the lesson', its pace, rather than about finding gaps in knowledge through misconceptions.

The only point at which Amy and Jane mentioned questioning was when they were asked about it. For Amy her only comment on questioning was that she used them to, 'clarify[ing] a lot, recapping. I did the recap bit via questioning initially' (Amy) and for Jane, in the same interview, 'I think clarifying'. Both replies are fairly characteristic of English lessons where teachers begin the class by asking for a recall of what had happened in the previous lesson be it a book they had studied or an activity they had engaged in. Clarification may also mean the type of question that Peter asked – questions about plot and character or they may be simply clarifying instructions. These questions may be comparatively closed in nature, particularly if they come at the start of a lesson, but in a way they are not the main focus of the lesson. If they are simply making clear what has to be done then the subsequent tasks will show whether or not they have understood the instruction. If they are recall questions – they are just a means of getting everyone's attention. The brevity of Amy and Jane's response in answer to a question on questions, shows that to them they might be seen as unimportant.

For Morag, she could only think that she used questions occasionally as a disciplinary device. 'Sometimes I use questioning as a technique for bringing off-task behaviour back on task' (Morag). It is significant that she used the word 'task' because this was the main way she questioned pupils, through task. Yet she had to be reminded that she questioned the pupils at all and this she only did when it was pointed out that in some ways tasks were the way English teachers posed questions. 'If I set up a task, yes, I'll quite often have, on a sheet of paper, what they've got to do, if that's what you mean and then they work their way through it. So it is questioning I suppose. Yes it is. LAUGHS' (Morag). Her laughter here is telling as it could be seen that again asking specific questions of her pupils is less significant than getting them involved in a task. It is this activity that promotes the kind of thinking time that Black and Wiliams (1998b) speak of. They introduced the notion of thinking time because the average wait time for answering questions was 0.8 of a minute (Rowe, 1974), which is, for many pupils, insufficient for them to think of an answer. Giving them more time to think, when answering, was seen to be beneficial. But far from the teacher waiting a little longer pupils are able to discuss a task at length. 'It's directing them to explore a bit further than they might have already isn't it. You can set up a task and it's usual to explore it further' (Morag). What is interesting is that she emphasizes exploration as a result of the task rather than answering questions per se, adding that 'it's usual to explore it further'; it is the common occurrence. Tasks are where you probe an issue a bit further.

With Peter this amounts to feedback. He says, of a low ability, Year 11 class,

> I do use their feedback an awful lot because then at the end of it I have to rake through what we've got in terms of understanding. And then that adjusts my level at which I'm teaching it or the type of assignments that I set. So in a sense I am letting them determine what it is they are going to write because I know how difficult it is for a lot of them to write. So I make sure that I've listened to what they've understood and then modelled things around that. (Peter)

His response is interesting in a number of ways. To begin with he adjusts how he teaches according to how much they have understood, 'that adjusts my level at which I'm teaching'. This is what formative assessment is about. Black and Wiliam's definition of formative assessment is

> all those activities undertaken by teachers, *and by their students in assessing themselves,* which provide information to be used as feedback to modify the teaching and learning activities in which they are engaged. *Such assessment becomes 'formative assessment' when the evidence is actually used to adapt the*

teaching work to meet the needs. (Black and Wiliam, 1998b, p. 2; emphasis in original)

Peter is taking what the pupils have to say, how they 'feedback' to him, and altering his teaching accordingly. But this does not mean he dumbs down what they learn. In a comment he made previously, he says,

So I use the feedback to try and actually beat my Year 11 over the head with their responses. I say 'Look you answered this, you had a fantastic answer about Lennie [a character in *Of Mice and Men*], you know, you understand him completely and now you are refusing to write about it'. (Peter)

So although he modifies his teaching, he attempts to encourage his students to write positively, telling them all the time that, for example they had a 'fantastic answer' and that they 'understand him completely'. What Peter understands is that it is 'difficult for a lot of them to write' and this is significant too because he prioritizes what they understand over technical difficulties. He explains, 'They're brilliant at talking to me but won't write anything . . . You've got the whole nervousness, often, about writing and committing it to paper and spelling and all the other things they worry about' (ibid.). It is in speaking that they give 'fantastic answers' and that is what is important.

He also, in effect, lets them 'determine what it is they are going to write' because he has 'listened to what they've understood and then modelled things around that'. The writing task is determined by how much Peter has understood about what the pupils have learned and, too, by the pupils articulating what they need and understand as well. Armed with this information Peter goes about modelling the writing for them. He does not have a pre-planned writing model, which he gives the pupils, but one that is worked out in conjunction with the class. Again this is very much formative practice, for according to Black and Wiliam, as we have seen, '*Such assessment becomes "formative assessment" when the evidence is actually used to adapt the teaching work to meet the needs*' (Black and Wiliam, 1998b, p. 2).

This constitutes the kind of dialogue that should be essential to formative assessment. As Black and Wiliam point out, 'All such work involves some degree of feedback between those taught and the teacher, and this is entailed in the quality of the interaction which is at the heart of pedagogy' (ibid., p. 16). It is possible, therefore, that this is why most of the English teachers either positively objected to or simply disregarded some techniques that were introduced to encourage the KMOFAP teachers to adopt formative practices.

One such technique was the practice of not asking for hands to be put up when answering questions. The rationale for doing this was partly that a teacher would not get the 'right' answers from a small number of volunteers and also that the class realized that anyone could be asked to answer a question and thus the dialogue would be more inclusive. For Morag it was worth contemplating. Having been at an inset sessions run by the maths and science departments, who were advocating it as a method, she had thought about it but had not actually put it into practice.

> I don't make them sit on their hands, no . . . But I, I think children automatically put their hands up when you ask a question but I don't automatically ask a child who has got their hand up. I might ask one who hasn't. (Morag)

It would seem that her practice already incorporated the rationale for no hands up. Daniel had tried the technique of no hands up and found it a disaster.

> I tried it with the group you saw today and they were like – doing what? And it was like I'd said, 'Good morning children and today I'm going to cut your feet off with a blunt bread knife.' It was like, you know, it was like something had gone wrong. (Daniel)

One pupil explained why they so objected to a no hands up class.

> He put his hand, and I said, 'No put your hand down' and he said, 'You are restricting our freedom of speech. We want to say things to you about what you are talking about and we are not allowed to put our hand up.' It doesn't work, because it's not like a – two plus two equals. It's because kids, it's kind of, it's sort of an interactive thing more. It's social, in a way, it's social. (ibid.)

Here Daniel is differentiating his class from, say, a maths class. In a maths class, he seems to be saying there are right answers. In his class participating is more 'social', there is no right and wrong answer so that putting one's hands up was simply a form of turn taking. They all wanted to have a say and having your hand up indicated this. He added that sometimes asking someone who didn't have their hand up and was just gazing out of the window might be a good thing, but he added, 'Looking around you of course you all put your hands up very regularly and therefore that's a complete waste of time' (ibid.) He concluded,

> And I couldn't stop them putting their hands up because they want to butt in. It's like being in a conversation. If we are sitting here and you are doing it because you

in charge of the conversation, but if this was a kind of chatty, social conversation and I appointed myself chair and said 'What would you like to say at this point in the conversation'. No. 'What would you like to say at this point.' You know, it's not normal. (ibid.)

What Daniel is trying to create in his classroom, then, and has to an extent succeeded in getting it, is 'social conversation'. A no hands up policy would interfere with the way in which the 'conversation' went. This in many respects is the kind of dialogic classroom that Robin Alexander speaks of and wishes to encourage in his booklet *Towards Dialogic Teaching: Rethinking classroom talk* (Alexander, 2006a). Ultimately, Alexander,

Requires willingness and skill to engage with minds, ideas and ways of thinking other than our own; it involves the ability to question, listen, reflect, reason, explain, speculate and explore ideas . . . [it] lays the foundations not just of successful learning but also social cohesion, active citizenship and the good society. (Alexander, 2006b, p. 5)

And while this may not precisely describe the kinds of 'conversation' that goes on in Daniel's classroom it is nearer this kind of dialogue than the traditional teacher/ response scenario that a hands down policy is trying to discourage. Daniel and Morag have not then failed to put into practice an important AfL technique, rather they have considered the greater question of what makes formative assessment work and enabled it to happen in their classes.

Peer assessment and sharing the criteria with the learner

Perhaps the biggest divergence of practice, however, came in the form of peer assessment. The maths and science teachers had come on to peer assessment quite late in the process and had looked more at the role of questioning. But for English teachers peer assessment was already something that they did and so they began here. Their frequent use of peer assessment in English possibly owes something of its origins to the National Writing Project (NWP), of the eighties, which made considerable use of the technique, and this was in large part thanks to the work of Vygotsky. In essence the belief of the NWP, and so of Vygotsky, was that reading other people's work was a kind of enactment of the ZPD. Through reading another's work one could see both how someone else had done the task and in what way we had completed it ourselves. For

Peter peer assessment 'completely sidelined' him as a teacher, a move which he felt was beneficial.

> Their engagement with peers is, I think, always impressive. And you know they get a great deal out of it . . . And I'm quite often, in that particular instance, the class is also getting ideas about these images and there's a kind of mutual understanding building, going on in that situation. (Peter)

What he describes is the kind of social interaction that James talks of in her definition of social constructivism where the teacher has created 'an environment in which people can be stimulated to think and act' (James, 2009, p. 57), and which 'learning is by definition a social and collaborative activity in which people develop their thinking together' (ibid., p. 57). His class develop a 'mutual understanding' that he believes is 'always impressive'.

Morag actually begins her interview by talking of peer assessment. 'This particular group have been used to marking their own work, to peer assessment. They've been doing it for at least two years, since I've had them so they're used to doing this'. She goes on to add, however, that it is 'Only really this year that they've also been doing it with the [GCSE] criteria in front of them' (Morag).

It is a technique she also uses in the lower school.

> I think it works because they really focus on the task in front of them. They quite enjoy looking at other people's work for a variety of reasons and I think it makes them aware, when they look at other people's work, things they might have done themselves or might not have done in their own work. (Morag)

These 'readings' might help us improve our work as a social interaction and this is in essence what Morag says she uses peer assessment for. All the other comments, which she then goes onto make, are organizational. She has concerns, for example, about whether or not a child will be humiliated.

> If there is a child whose work is of such a weak standard that I think he might be humiliated by having someone who is not really sensitive looking at his work . . . I would perhaps carefully decide that I will look at the child's work myself. And I have done that. There are some children who I think might be unkind.

But even here the child's work is read. All of the teacher's involved say at some point that they have used peer assessment. Emily, for example, says 'I've always liked peer assessment and peer marking, so I mean, at the moment the way I'm working is very much the way I've always worked' (Emily). She links her use of peer assessment to progress

> I've done that with GCSE groups and with these little uns. Get them to read their work, read somebody, paired work, read somebody else's work, assess it. I also get them to do – read my work, what do you think? Which are the good bits . . . Year 11 really enjoy that . . . so that's helped them, I think, with their creative writing especially . . . [They] try and concentrate. Ooh somebody said that and it was really good. And it really changed them and gave them a real boost. (Emily)

What is interesting is that she includes her own writing in the peer assessment exercise. Whereas Morag would look at an individual's writing if she felt the class would not mark it fairly, Emily goes one stage further. Although she says that they do not like to criticize her work, saying, for example, that her Year 11 group 'enjoy looking for the best bits rather than – where could you do better?' (Emily), she is still asking them to consider her work, entering it into the community of interpreters. Again this enacts Mary James definition of 'learning' in her classroom, for it too, like Peter, is a 'social and collaborative activity in which people develop their thinking together' (James, 2009, p. 57).

Classroom practice

Peer assessment

Before we go on to look at the Learning how to Learn Project, in the next chapter, we should examine some of the classroom practice that went on as part of KMOFAP. We will look at only two – the first is an example of peer assessment, the second a look at classroom dialogue. Both take place in Kate and Daniel's school, though this does not mean that they had better examples, just that these are two that I have chosen because they exemplify, in part, some of what this project established about formative assessment.

The peer assessment is on the first draft of a piece of Year 10 coursework on Tybalt and Mercutio's deaths in *Romeo and Juliet*. This is in itself interesting for a number of reasons. To begin with it shows that there can be a link between the formative and summative. The coursework is used ultimately as a piece of summative assessment for GCSE. So this essay is being looked at formatively, through peer assessment, where the pupil can, as a result, improve on their work, and summatively for an examination. This is one of the reasons that many English teachers are worried about the new GCSE. Although there is a course-based element all the work done has to be done in controlled conditions which can be, in effect, mini exams. This means that, for example, you cannot take in any work done previously in class so that you could not take a peer-assessed essay into the exam and make improvements on what you had written. We shall look further at the new GCSE in Chapter 8.

To return to the essay on Romeo and Juliet, here the intention is that the pupil will read the comments made on their piece of work and rewrite it. I have only put the peer comments and not the essay itself but it was photocopied onto a piece of A3 paper and the comments were written down both sides of the essay.

Yr 10 Example of peer assessment	Essay	Points not numbered in original
1. Lots of points blended together. It gets confusing without any		6. Too brief 'Mercutio wants to fight' . . . 'then they were fighting'. You need more info and emotions in between what causes them to fight do they threaten each other first.
2. This sentence doesn't work well. You can't use two becauses in a sentence		7. Good explanations an emotions
Too many ands		8. Good thoughts and opinions from Romeo on the situation
3. A bit vague. Mercutio doesn't just die, he suffered. Maybe add some quotes from Mercutio		9. I like this bit when he says 'it was over' you could maybe add finally into to describe how glad he is for it to be over.
4. Good choise [sic] of words. They are good to describe Romeo's feelings		10. Lots of good points. Everything is included. Try to space out all of the events instead of blending them all together. This makes it a bit confusing to read. Second half a lot better than the first half
5. More descriptive bits for Tybalts death not just he fell over dead		

What is most impressive about this piece of peer assessment is the range and type of comments. In some respects this is suggestive of the kind of assessment that is done on pupils' work in general. Pupils learn to peer assess through constant modelling as well as practice. In order for them to peer assess well, the teacher must also assess in detail for them to see what good assessment is like. But more fundamentally, through their assessment and their teaching, this teacher appears to have begun to share their 'guild knowledge' of the subject. What you have here, therefore, possibly unarticulated, is the beginnings of the pupil's understanding of what that guild knowledge of the subject looks like in practice.

The English teacher must make a variety of remarks that shows a holistic view of English and the assessment process in particular. The peer markers' comments then pick up on this. They make technical comments but also talk about the overall shape of the essay. In fact the first and last points they make are about clarity. Their first comment is, 'Lots of points blended together. It gets confusing' and this is echoed in the last point too, 'Lots of good points. Everything is included. Try to space out all of the events instead of blending them all together. This makes it a bit confusing to read. Second half a lot better than the first half'.

This is not quite teacher speak but very close. One knows what the peer marker is trying to say when they comment on points 'blended'. It is quite an interesting turn of phrase. They do not say overlap, which is a comment that might be made by a teacher, but blended. The image of a blender mixing in all the points would indeed be 'confusing'. It would blur things to the point of a disparate mush. What they ask for is 'to space out all of the events'. In other words they are to separate them, giving clarity. In some respects this peer assessor is similar to the LATE markers almost 50 years ago.

Indeed they go on to say what you might add in 'spac[ing] out all the events'. On three separate occasions they talk about how the author might add to what they have written. Comments three, five and six are concerned with a more detailed look at how characters feel about events, what motivates them. This, in a tentative way, shows the peer marker's view of the importance of subject knowledge and it is two fold. They argue that you can tell what a character is thinking or feeling and that it is what they say that gives you this information. And once more, to add such information would prevent the point from being 'a bit vague' and give it clarity. Clarity then, works at the level of subject knowledge as well as overall structure.

So for example, 'Mercutio doesn't just die, he suffered'. In order to demonstrate that this is true the author should, 'Maybe add some quotes from Mercutio'.

The word 'suffered' is also telling. It shows that the peer assessor recognizes a degree of anguish on the character's part that is derived from the text, hence 'add some quotes'. Or again the description on the fight between Mercutio and Tybalt is 'Too brief'. The peer assessor tells the author to add 'more info and emotions' and in so doing requires them to examine the text further, to see, 'What causes them to fight do they threaten each other first'.

This sense of engagement with the characters, but a realization that such knowledge must be found in the text, demonstrates the way in which the teacher must have imparted guild knowledge both through the way she taught and assessed. It is even true of the technical comments that the peer assessor gives, for they do not stop at the technical. In point two they write that there are 'two many ands' and 'becauses'. To begin with they appear to be making a point about repetition, though the word is not used. But this is elaborated on 'It doesn't make the sentence work well'. Here the peer assessor is possibly developing an ear for language, for what does work well as well as what does not. It may be confusing to the reader but also it does not sound right and this is, perhaps, what is important.

Ironically, it is the way criteria in English all 'blend together' that make it, on the one hand so hard to assess, and on the other can make peer assessment so effective. Significantly the teacher has not singled out any particular criterion for the peer assessor to look at but has just asked them to comment on what they read. Confronted with this the author of the piece will have a good commentary on their essay, including positive comments like 'Good choise [sic] of words. They are good to describe Romeo's feelings'. These will give the author a better idea of what to build on when the peer assessor makes suggestions as to what might be improved.

Although it is not possible to know what effect this had on the peer assessor themselves, one can tentatively presume that they may have learned something about how an essay is presented as well, that they will have seen the importance of putting in quotes and description and that they have begun to learn why, that they are gaining in guild knowledge.

Dialogue

The first thing that should be noted about this lesson is that Kate, the teacher, is using a model of English which privileges the engagement of the pupils with the meaning of the poem, and the author's voice, over the acquisition and application of technical terminology. What will become evident, however, is that this not an 'anything goes' response but one which is carefully structured to extend pupils thinking about a text.

The lesson was undertaken by a top set Year 11 class as part of their work on the AQA anthology. They had already looked at some of Carol-Ann Duffy's poems and were now turning their attention to the poem 'Before You Were Mine'. Kate, the class teacher, had taught this poem the year before and had noted that pupils found the concept of the poet writing as herself but before she was born, difficult to grasp. To this end, as preparation for the lesson, she had asked the pupils to interview their parents about their lives before they, the pupils, had been born. The homework was designed to enable the pupils to begin to enter the imaginative space occupied by the premise of Duffy's poem. Given that this activity was a response to Kate's previous experience of teaching the poem, and the difficulties that she had observed in those pupils, the homework was, in itself an example of the formative use of feedback. She had altered her teaching to meet the pupils' needs.

The pupils were asked to discuss their findings in groups of four. This created seven groups within the class. The experience was clearly revelatory for many of the pupils, particularly when they had looked at photos of their much younger parents. The seventies clothing of many of these young adults appeared surprisingly acceptable to the 'grungers' in the class. At this point Kate moved through the class and listened into the discussion without commenting at all. After approximately seven minutes she called the class to attention and introduced Duffy's poem, which she read aloud. She then asked the pupils, still in their groups, to reread the poem and relate it to the activity in which they had just engaged.

At this point Kate again began to move between the groups. The pattern was always the same. She would hover on the edge for a few minutes, listening to the conversation and then intervene either with a comment or a question: 'Unusual perspective in this poem'; 'Whose is it?' 'Interesting perspective isn't it'; 'How does it relate to the poem?'; 'Yep that's where we could go next'; 'You'll be looking at that in more detail in a minute'. Each of these comments and prompts, therefore represents a reponse to something said by a pupil.

Some represent confirmation of ideas – the 'unusual' or 'interesting perspective'. Others are designed to develop thinking, 'Whose is it?' or 'How does it relate to the poem?' Others indicate that the pupils' thinking is already going beyond the parameters of the task – 'Yep that's where we could go next' 'You'll be looking at that in more detail in a minute'. After around seven minutes on this activity Kate addressed the class as a whole with the following question

'Why have I asked you to do this?', to which a pupil, at her request responded, 'Because the perspective of the poem is odd'. Turning to another pupil who had not raised her hand Kate asked, 'What is it Victoria?' to which she replied 'She's talking as herself but before she was born'.

This exchange was prompted by a closed question, but one which interestingly drew attention to the intentions of the teacher in the construction of the task. It acted as both a recap and summary on the group discussions, reinforcing both the purpose and content of what had been learned in this section. In addition, Kate used this very brief exchange as a transition point within the lesson. Her response to Victoria's observation was 'Yes interesting' adding that such a perspective was indeed unusual and that they were now going to look at the poem in more depth to understand that perspective better. To this end she asked them to split their groups in half and re-read the poem with a view to identifying those ideas on which they would like clarification or development from Duffy. In particular Kate asked them to look at the 'connotations' of what Duffy was writing, checking first that they knew what 'connotation' meant.

Again as the pupils settled to the task Kate circulated the class, listened to the discussion and intervened within the discussion. On average she made around four interventions per pair. What is interesting about the interventions is that they vary considerably, all are impromptu, each constituting a response to the pupils' thinking. In this way the interventions act as formative feedback, as defined by Black and Wiliam, in that Kate is using the evidence of the pupils' responses to meet their needs. She is also echoing teachers like Daniel or Peter in their use of questions. It is a genuine enquiry. Below is a sample of the dialogue, where I have focused, for the purposes of the discussion, on the nature of the teacher's interventions.

What is interesting to note is the way in which Kate's interactions with some pairs are considerably more directed than others, suggesting that she believes some pairs need more guidance than others. In this way, also, Kate differentiated within the class through the type of interventions she made. These range from the demand that the pupils actually get on with the work, as in pair five, through closely structured exchanges, as with pair two and six, to the more open prompts in pair eight.

Pair 1
'What do you think?' – pupil replies.
'She could be', pupil responds.

'Right that's what I mean by unusual perspective. You don't really write about something before you were born.'
'Don't get hung up on the first line.'

Pair 2
'Any other reasons why she's comparing her mother to Marylin?' Pupil responds.
'Anything else? Think about her representation.' Another pupil responds
'Think about how her public viewed her', pauses then prompts, 'She's famous'.
'So why compare her mother?' Pupils respond and are led to idea that she's an 'icon of the age'.

Pair 3
'You're raising a question aren't you. Write that down as your first question.'
'No there are no answers – perhaps the group will help you.'
'How will you phrase it/Is that what you mean.'

Pair 4
A boy talks at length and Kate responds, 'How?' The pupil continues his train of thought and Kate ends the exchange by commenting, 'Think you might be reading too much into it.'

Pair 5
'Not much annotation going on.' She then listens again and adds, 'You want to look at this one' before moving on.

Pair 6
'What's the comparison that's being set up?'
'Good question.' 'Is it?'
'We don't usually think . . . '
'Why does she say? . . . What's the point of the simile?' Pupil responds
'I mean if you think about it the five senses.'
'I mean do you not associate people with scent.' Pupil responds.
'So, an unusual simile.'

Pair 7
'Is this what? That could be one of your questions.'
'I'm not going to tell you what to think.' Pupil responds.
'Yes that's exactly what she's saying – that's why its a good question to ask.'

Pair 8
Looks over their shoulder.
'That's very interesting any other connotations with that word.' This prompts several responses.

Interestingly she does steer them away from certain avenues of interpretation – 'Don't get too hung up on the first line' and 'Think you might be reading too much into it', while at the same time encouraging open responses, as with pairs seven and eight. To an extent these exchanges illustrate a tension within English teaching between a desire for openness and originality of response as against understanding and appreciating a shared reading of a text. What I want to argue is that this tension, when handled well, is a very creative, possibly essential dynamic. There is, however, a fine line between over and under direction within that tension. In a sense maintaining that very fine line is part of the skill of the formative teacher and is dependent on their assessment of the pupils' responses and subsequent feedback. As Dylan Wiliam and Paul Black remark, 'All such work involves some degree of feedback between those taught and the teacher, and this is entailed in the quality of the interaction which is at the heart of pedagogy' (Black and Wiliam, 1998a, p. 16).

The tension between openness and a desire to direct, as outlined above, extended into the next activity the class undertook. This came after about ten minutes of the paired discussions. At this point Kate intervened and asked the whole class to, 'Write down your questions before you forget them. There are some very interesting questions'. She then returned to a selection of the pairs, briefly adding comments such as those to pair 7, 'It's an interesting theory – one I don't subscribe to. Look at other stuff in the poem now'. After a time check to the whole class, Kate returned to pair 6 to say, 'Pose that question but you'll need evidence'.

Again, in the case of one pair she has redirected their attention and called upon her own authority to encourage them to look at other issues, while with the other pair she allowed an interpretation but required more evidence. In both interventions she is using her own judgement about how to interpret the poem to guide the pupils' reading. Yet in each case she is assessing where they are and where they need to be, through their comments, to determine the type of intervention she makes in order to develop their thinking. In effect the way she has constructed the task has allowed the pupils to make their own readings, her interventions simply require them either to deepen these readings or explore other avenues that will further develop their ideas.

The multiplicity of comments the pupils make in response to the poem mean that it is more helpful to consider their progression as towards a horizon, rather than a defined goal (Marshall, 2004a). This is because their starting points and responses are so different. So that while, as a teacher, Kate can foresee the generality of the interpretations the pupils might make, and indeed use this foresight to create activities designed to ensure that they grasp meanings she wants them to understand, she cannot know how they will express these responses, and thus make those responses their own. Nor can she predict what else they may glean from the poem that she had not foreseen.

To an extent what appears to be happening is that through the process of discussion pupils are, again, being apprenticed into a kind of guild knowledge about ways of responding to a poem. The teacher has a notion of quality and how that is made manifest in the poem but crucially, as we shall see, that guild knowledge includes the notion of originality and individuality of response. Her interventions indicate to the pupils that she believes some directions are more fruitful than others. Yet, as we shall see, she does not rely on her guidance alone but uses the pupils themselves to assess the quality of the interpretation of their classmates in what, in effect, is a form of peer assessment.

To begin with, five minutes after the first whole class intervention, Kate put the pairs back into the same groups of four that in which they had began the lesson and asked them to concentrate on answering the questions they had posed as pairs. She gave them seven minutes and again went to each of the groups in turn. On this occasion she only made interventions with around half the groups being content with the rest simply to listen to their discussion. In this way she enabled the pupils to assess, evaluate and develop the responses they had made to the poem.

At the end of this section of the lesson she brought the whole class back together. The questions she then asked of the pupils, and the issues which she raised were based on what she had observed, emerging from their discussion. She used this evidence, further to develop and shape their thinking. But again she built on the pupils' responses to do this rather than imposing a predetermined checklist which the pupils then applied.

The pattern she followed tended to be to select an individual from one group to pose a question and then identify another group who had also looked at this issue to respond. For example, when she asked one group for their question, they replied, 'We looked at the idea of being not wanted'. Kate then referred this observation across the class to another group who had come up with the same idea. 'Can you help?' 'Look at the tone of the poem'. This prompted a number of responses some of which were very sophisticated including the observation that 'maybe she's exploring the difference between her parental and glamorous life'.

Another exchanged followed the same pattern. A group asked, 'Is she writing after the mother has dies?' Kate responded, 'Yes a number of you asked this – 'why do you ask?' to which the pupil replied, 'She changes tense'. Kate then threw this observation back to the rest of the class by asking 'Can you help anyone'. Again this prompted some fascinating responses including the idea that 'We thought that meant she could see her mother through the makeup' and a boy who observed that it was a bit like quantum mechanics in that it was all relative depending on the perspective. The lesson ended after this final exchange.

In a sense this lesson is illustrative of the creative dynamic arising from the tension between a teacher's desire to guide pupils' thinking while at the same time wanting to encourage their own response. It is this element of the lesson that casts further light on the nature of guild knowledge. This is because the progress of the lesson suggests that entry into the guild is a process which can accommodate variety, precisely because an element of that guild knowledge is the individuality and originality of response.

As we have seen, even though the way she shaped the discussion was dependent on her own reading of the poem, the activities Kate designed facilitated the pupils' own responses to the poem. The fact that she indicated that certain paths, to mix metaphors slightly, were actually blind alleys, meant that the pupils went on to generate other ideas which were expressed in a manner that was unique to the pupils, for example 'maybe she's exploring the difference between her parental and glamorous life'. Moreover they created interpretations that she herself had not considered. This was true of the response about the mother and her makeup and even more so the observation about quantum mechanics. Significantly, then, the class became a place for these original interpretations to be shared because of the approach she adopted.

Another way of analysing what is going on in this lesson, however, is by considering the way in which the pupils' thinking is scaffolded and developed by the activities that have been planned. This builds on Black and Wiliam's observation about 'the quality of the interaction which is at the heart of pedagogy' (Black and Wiliam, 1998b, p. 16). Kate's lesson is illustrative of this. Her tasks provide 'organised and structure learning experiences and opportunities' to extend pupils thinking in the general direction she wishes them to pursue. She uses pair work and group discussion to develop the pupils' understanding of the poem, through 'social interaction, negotiation and shared learning'. The final section of the lesson reinforces the 'communal' nature of the learning.

Moreover as the 'tutor' she guides their thinking in the way in which she prompts, questions and frames the discussion and, too, by the way she calls upon other members of the class, 'peers', to contribute. In so doing she is negotiating their path through the ZPD. As we have seen, for Cordon the 'key factors in determining children's learning "potential" will be the nature of the discourse and the quality of teacher intervention' and such interaction for Black and Wiliam lies 'at the heart of pedagogy'. For as we have seen again, there is a fine line between over and under direction in a lesson. It is here that the work of Perrenoud, and his concept of the regulation of learning, is helpful in developing our understanding as to the nature of that interaction.

In his response to Black and Wiliam's paper on formative assessment Philippe Perrenoud argues that the notion of feedback itself is insufficient to understand its place in developing learning, or rather it needs to be set in the broader conceptual framework of the regulation of learning. Crucial to his notion of what this means is the idea that 'regulation does not include setting up activities suggested to, or imposed on, the pupils but their adjustment once they have been initiated' (Perrenoud, 1998, p. 88). He goes on to suggest that 'traditional school exercises are not regulated in the same way as more open ended activities such as research or projects' (ibid., p. 88). In extending this he draws conclusions about the limitation of criteria which by now have become familiar. Describing a 'traditional' approach he writes,

> Traditional teaching inevitably reduces its regulation to its simplest expression . . . The ensuing retroactive regulation is often limited to reworking notions which 'have not been fully understood by a significant proportion of the pupils'. Formative evaluation is confined to temporary microsummative evaluation, followed by remediation.
>
> The regulatory influence of formative evaluation is weak if it is limited to subsequent criterion referenced evaluation which, at the end of a phase of teaching, highlights gaps in knowledge, errors and insufficient grasp of the subject, leading to remediation. (ibid., p. 91)

Such an approach is reminiscent of the crude rather than sophisticated deployment of the strategies suggested by Myhill, who writes on grammar for writing (QCA, 1999) and the advocates of genre theory (see Christie and Misson). Perrenoud, however, argues that while such feedback is better than nothing it is limited because it only takes place at the end of the sequence of learning. Instead, he suggests we should go for a more interactive model where the regulation takes place 'during the activity through an exchange with the pupil (face to face or in a group)' (1998, p. 91). And this is particularly in evidence in Kate's lesson. Feedback is integral to this activity. Perrenoud goes on to point out, however, that the task itself is crucial to creating an environment in which that intervention will be most meaningful and in which the effects of that intervention will be maximized.

He also asserts, like Black and Wiliam, that feedback is of little or no use unless it is understood by the learner. So that, despite the feedback being appropriate – the way in which it is communicated, the moment in time in which it is offered, even the mood or receptivity of the pupil – will have a bearing on whether that feedback is internalized and the pupils learn. In other words at no point does he offer simple solutions to what he describes as the highly complex world of the classroom.

But the notion of the regulation of learning provides a language of description or mechanism by which we can understand how teachers might negotiate the ever shifting the demands of the 'scaffold' as, 'each new task will generate a different ZPD' (Corden, 2000, p. 8). To do so, however, it may be worth applying the 'regulation of learning' to the interactive dynamic of the classroom and teacher interventions, and use the term 'scaffolding' to refer to something conceived prior to the lesson. For in separating out these two elements it might be possible to see more clearly how they combine to provide feedback for the pupils. Moreover while the way in which a teacher chooses to 'scaffold' the learning in his or her lesson is undoubtedly part of the regulatory process, it would probably be true to say that English teachers generally associate it with the planning stage.

In other words they may well consider what they wish the pupils to learn and then, working backwards, create activities that would support that learning. Or as Perrenoud might describe it, they try to ensure that the environment maximizes the potential for any subsequent interventions to be meaningful. Once the lesson is underway they then 'regulate the learning' through a series of interventions. As Kate's lesson demonstrates the teacher's interventions need to be responsive to the way in which the pupils engage with the task.

Conclusion

The structuring or scaffolding of lessons, then, and the interventions that teachers make is significant. What governs those decisions and, perhaps, as, or more importantly, the beliefs that the teachers had, becomes important in the next chapter. For now it is worth noting that all these teachers took a holistic view of what they were doing and did not atomize English.

Assessment for Learning and Learning How to Learn

5

The Learning how to Learn Project (LHTL) was, in some ways, a natural extension of KMOFAP, the only difference being that it did not specifically focus on English. Many of the classrooms watched, however, and many of the teachers interviewed were English specialists. The project was set up in 2002 and it ran until 2006. It was a unique project and involved the Universities of Cambridge, King's, Reading and the Open University. Each university was given a particular responsibility for an aspect of the research. Cambridge was to look at schools, King's – classrooms and Reading and the Open University were to look at networks of schools, how schools and local authorities worked together. The overall focus of the research was how networks, schools and classrooms learned how to learn.

LHTL was part of a bigger overall project known as the Teaching and Learning Project which ran in three phases. LHTL was part of the second phase and all research had to be carried out between several universities. Most universities, despite being linked to an overall theme, tended to focus on their own individual research. LHTL differed in that all the universities involved worked together the whole time. Research, for example, carried out at school level had a direct impact on that done at classroom level.

It was, for King's, however, a continuation of KMOFAP because, in asking how individuals in classrooms learned how to learn, we were looking, once more, at assessment for learning. In essence we were asking how, if at all, AfL, and so learning how to learn could be rolled out and managed on a much bigger scale. In all we looked at 40 primary and secondary schools, so the kind of intense involvement that we had had during KMOFAP, with workshops, was no longer possible. Having said that, two schools, who had been involved in KMOFAP in Oxfordshire, were also involved in LHTL. In this respect there was some continuity. Other authorities included Hertfordshire, Essex, and Redbridge in London, as well as a Virtual Education Action Zone (VEAZ).

Schools were clustered together and an initial meeting, with whole schools present, was held. This was on the benefits of AfL. Schools were then asked to go away and develop practice that encouraged formative assessment in their classrooms. This they did in a wide variety of ways. Some set up specialist groups, others focused on peer assessment among teachers, seeing how well they were doing, others tried the whole list of techniques that were on offer, others still had members of the research team come in and give additional inset. This was because each school was given a 'critical friend' from the research team. Academics then had half a dozen or so schools that they worked with especially.

During this process the research became focused on two particular questions:

1. How can teachers and schools use AfL to promote LTHL, and especially learning autonomy, in their pupils within learning environments that they perceived as constraining, and what conditions facilitate innovation and change?
2. In this context, what is the relationship between changes in classroom practice and change in values and beliefs about learning? (James, et al. 2007)

Two things became evident that made it different from KMOFAP. The first was that although we were looking at classrooms, we were now looking at them in the context of the whole school. The second was that teachers' beliefs about learning had become important. The KMOFAP technique had been to discuss strategies, which involved AfL. It was hoped that the belief structure of the teachers, and a commitment to greater pupil autonomy, would follow. Paul Black and Dylan Wiliam called this the Trojan Horse of AfL (2006). In some respects this echoes the Literacy Hour Framework. Here the rationale was similar. If everybody were exposed to the literacy hour then eventually it would bring about change in teaching and learning. No one asked you to believe in the literacy hour, you just had to do what they advised.

With LTHL, however, we were being asked what teachers actually thought about the classes they taught and about how they thought pupils learned. In particular, as we shall see, we were asking how autonomous the pupils in lessons were and how autonomous the teachers wanted them to be. And, ultimately, whether or not this made a difference in their classrooms.

Crucial to appreciating the relevance of the teachers' understanding of learning to assessment is the notion of progression toward autonomy, and the teachers' role in facilitating this, through the activities in which they encourage pupils to engage. Most obvious, as we have already seen, is Vygotsky's concept of the ZPD. But significant, also, is Dewey's definition of 'progressive' education as 'high organization based upon ideas' (Dewey, 1966, p. 28–9); the challenge being, 'to discover and put into operation a principle of order and operation which follows from understanding what the educative experience signifies' (ibid., p. 29).

Dewey acknowledges that it is 'a difficult task to work out the kinds of materials, of methods, and of social relationships that are appropriate' (ibid., p. 29). In a sense this is what the teachers on the LH2L project were attempting to do. The implementation of AfL in the classroom, then, became about much more than the application of certain procedures – questioning, feedback, sharing the criteria with the learner and peer and self-assessment – it was about the realization of certain principles of teaching and learning. And this in part is what we have already seen in the last chapter, in particular through Kate's lesson.

Pupil autonomy

In some respects it may have been a good idea to ask the teachers in KMOFAP what they believed, as some of the points of controversy or difference from their maths and science colleagues may have been directly attributable to their beliefs about learning. There are strong hints, in what they say, of a belief in pupil autonomy. Daniel, for example, in his defence of having hands up in the classroom, as we have seen, quotes a child, and it is to the child's point of view that he gives preference.

'You are restricting our freedom of speech. We want to say things to you about what you are talking about and we are not allowed to put our hand up.' It doesn't work, because it's not like a – two plus two equals. It's because kids, it's kind of, it's sort of an interactive thing more. It's social, in a way, it's social. (Daniel)

The child has a mind their own and this needs to be respected. It is evident also if we look, once more, at some of Peter's comments about peer assessment. He says, for example,

Their engagement with peers is, I think, always impressive. And you know they get a great deal out of it . . . And I'm quite often, in that particular instance, the class is also getting ideas about these images and there's a kind of mutual understanding building, going on in that situation. (Peter)

He does not speak of his role as a teacher at all. In fact at another point in the interview he claims, as we have seen, ' I don't think I've ever taught anybody anything'. It is about the pupils' 'engagement', about their 'mutual understanding' and this is what is 'always impressive'. It is also as if in some way he is involved in the process. He starts by saying 'I'm quite often' but ends by saying 'the class is also getting ideas'. Again this shows the autonomy of the class, and, moreover, that in some respects, he is getting 'ideas' from them. At another point he talks of 'a natural rhythm of thought and a process of thought' and again ' a kind of internal dialogue'. All these speak of the pupils thinking for themselves and with each other.

Even Morag gestures towards the autonomous pupil: 'I think it makes them aware, when they look at other people's work, things they might have done themselves or might not have done in their own work.' Here peer assessment leads to self-assessment and it is not the teacher who decides what the pupils need to do but the pupils themselves.

The LHTL project

To return once more to the LHTL project, the move towards pupil autonomy as central to AfL came about through the school level research. As part of their research they had asked schools to complete a bi-variant questionnaire. All teachers were asked to comment on items, which, among other things, explored two things – their beliefs about learning and how they felt these were played out in practice. In so doing they identified practice/values gap (for a fuller discussion of this questionnaire see James and Pedder 2005). What is important to note is that these items were themselves grounded in the work on formative assessment undertaken by KMOFAP and, too, the principles for assessment for learning established by the Assessment Reform Group (2002).

Three robust orthogonal factors emerged from the questionnaire responses – Making Learning Explicit, Promoting Learning Autonomy and Performance Orientation. What they discovered was that Promoting Learning Autonomy was the most challenging aspect of practice to implement (James and Pedder, 2005). In all, only a fifth of the teachers believed that learning autonomy was promoted in practice as well as valued (see James and Pedder, 2006). This was echoed in the videos we watched, where again only around a fifth promoted learning autonomy.

In all 27 video recordings of lessons were watched. Almost all the lessons were filmed at the midpoint of the project and so provided snapshots of classroom practice. The three factors found in the questionnaire were used as a semi structured guide when analysing the lessons. To begin with they came from the same theoretical position that we were bringing to bear on the video data and too they arose out of the grounded observations of classroom practice from previous research projects such as KMOFAP and ARG. Finally the items had been validated and checked for reliability (see James and Pedder, 2005).

But the other way in which these videos were looked at was using Eisner's notion of connoisseurship (Eisner, 1991). Although his technique is more about actual classroom visits, and watching a video is not the same, nevertheless, a certain critique of the lessons was possible. Again, therefore, we took an arts view even of the data analysis. Eisner argues strongly that in much educational analysis the arts view, with an aim at the 'expansion of perception and the enlargement of understanding' (ibid., p. 113), is too often missing. This is what we were trying to do.

For classrooms are complex places. Lessons are difficult to analyse, even harder with a fixed camera placed at the back of the classroom so that some of the pupils' expressions cannot be seen and their work remains unanalysed. A video camera can also have a flattening effect. But a video is also an artefact, like watching a film and this is what English teachers, in theory, are good at, critiquing what they see or read. In the hurly-burly of such activity, then, we were trying to see if the lessons promoted pupil autonomy, 'to enlarge[ment] our understanding'. But we will return to the videos later.

The role of teachers' beliefs

The lesson as artefact?

For we also interviewed all those teachers whose lessons we watched and it is here that I want to begin, although we will only be talking about the English teachers who were interviewed and no one else. When analysing the interviews we focused on two aspects – their views on the promotion of learning autonomy, as this element had been central to the examination of the lessons, and their views on what might impede learning taking place.

What emerged from the data was a group of the teachers who, in some ways, viewed their lessons as an artefact which could be improved, crafted into something better. In other words, they did not see the lesson as something which was fixed or beyond their control but as something mutable over which they presided, an object which could be changed or transformed. And, as we will see, these teachers were the teachers who tried to give pupils the most autonomy. It is as if they translated their thoughts on their own autonomous role in the classroom to the pupils.

One of those interviewed, who belonged in this group, was Angela. She had a strongly held a conviction that her job was to make her classes less passively dependent on her and more dependent on themselves and each other. Angela's beliefs about learning all centred around a move towards the greater pupil independence. Yet running like a leit motif through her interview is the phrase, 'If I've taught a lesson, then I'll go over it, reflect, think, what could I do better next time?' And again, 'So I do a lesson with one and then I think, okay, how could I improve that for the next time?' (Angela)

> But it depends, sometimes it's just a thought and sometimes I actually kind of go back over the scheme of work, look at the lesson plan and write notes to myself for next time. So it depends on what it is really and how severely bad it went. (Angela)

Not all Angela's reflections are negative: 'I suppose you say what do you do better, but you can also say, what went well' (ibid.).

It is evident in Angela's comments that nothing in the classroom is fixed or beyond her control. It is the place where she needs to learn about how well she has done in relationship to the task she set herself – that of the pupils' learning. Her approach finds echoes in Carol Dweck. In her book *Self Theories* psychologist Dweck (2000) observes two contrasting and complementary views learning. She compares what she calls task versus ego involvement with learning and incremental versus entity theories of learning. Broadly speaking those who hold an entity theory of learning tend to view factors such as intelligence as fixed. Those who hold an incremental view of learning tend to believe, crudely, that learning more makes you smarter. Similarly those who focus on the task are more able to learn form the experience the task has given them and improve as a result than those who are 'ego' involved. This latter group appear impeded by focusing on issues such as their view of their own ability or the circumstances in which the task is undertaken.

All the lessons given by Angela, however, are experiences from which she can refine and develop her craft for the benefit of the pupils. It is this essentially progressive process – the possibility that all performance and knowledge can be developed – that Angela wishes her pupils to understand. In this way there is a synergy between her concept of independent learning and of the formative process for her pupils and the way she approaches her own teaching.

Even Fran, another of the teachers interviewed, views her teaching as something alterable.

> The idea that sometimes you prepare the lesson, which isn't appropriate for the pupils. It's over their head or it's too easy and that sometimes prevents learning from taking place, or meaningful learning . . . You might be able to control the situations so they complete the task but they haven't actually learnt anything because it's too complicated and they didn't get the hang of it or it was too easy and it was something they could dash off. (Fran)

By contrast, some of the teachers interviewed seem to hold a much more ego or entity view of what they are doing. It ought to be noted that the interviews took place at the midpoint of the project and some people changed their views, including Sheila (see Coffey, Sato and Thiebault, 2005). So although Sheila was on a trajectory of change at this stage her views seem quite fixed. To begin she only comments on the notion of pupil autonomy in one section of the interview. As a stated aim, therefore, it is far less dominant.

What is perhaps more interesting though, is the way in which Sheila articulates the notion of pupil autonomy and how she relates this to her role in the classroom. While stressing the importance of her relationship with the class she sees her role as 'focusing on my pupils' a use of the possessive that suggests a proprietorial and so hierarchical relationship with her class. Its perspective is very redolent of Miss Jean Brodie, who famously talked of 'my girls' and is more often connected with a traditional style of teaching. That Sheila is keen to distance herself from this approach to teaching, however, is evident in her interview in the section on pupil autonomy. She describes her perception of the pupils' attitudes towards learning:

> A lot of them see learning as being taught and their parents see learning as being taught.
>
> Interviewer: What does that mean, learning as being taught?
>
> S: The teacher delivers, the child takes note. The old fashioned ideas, the content. The teacher teaches and therefore the child is automatically going to learn because the teacher is standing at the front of the room delivering and we all know that that is not the case. They have to be involved, they have to be active learners so they learn, they are beginning to learn through group work, they are beginning to learn that discussion helps them, that talking to other people helps focus what they are thinking. They will talk now to each other without having to be told 'now you can talk to each other'. (Sheila)

The difficulty is that, despite her desire to change the role of the teacher, and the pupils' perception of that role, her attitudes towards toward the learner and learning, unlike Angela, are still quite fixed.

> The ones that do it are ready to get feedback, are ready to reassess their targets, and are ready to move on. The ones that don't do it, don't get the feedback, because there is nothing for me to discuss with them, and that's the biggest barrier they are actually bone idle, that group.
>   There are others who will do it but I think their biggest barrier is often their lack of confidence. Some of them it's a lack of language, but lack of confidence and inability to be independent. (Sheila)

In comparison with Angela, there is, in Sheila's response, less of a sense of how she can effect change in the classroom environment. The onus is on the pupils' readiness for independence rather than on her creating that readiness. Thus in some ways the failure is not hers, or rather, she can do little about it.

Yet her proprietorial attitude toward the class means that she feels a sense of ownership and responsibility to help the pupils. They are 'her' class. Ironically, the combination of these two factors – her belief in the pupils' lack of readiness and her sense of responsibility – lead her back into becoming the 'old-fashioned' teacher she wishes to avoid being. This is because she ends up doing much of the work for them to compensate for their lack. As we shall see later, in her lesson, she is anxious to spell out, at every point, what the pupils need to do. Her belief in the class's laziness and her absence of a sense of their readiness leads her to interrogate them until they have understood what she believes they must do to succeed. Independence becomes an added bonus not a stated aim.

Exams are also an extreme irritant.

> It all gets in the way. Exam courses, being tied to rules and regulations. Being tied to a set syllabus, because a lot of what is on the curriculum is not applicable to a lot of these kids and we could make them much better learners if we could be more creative in the way we use the curriculum and now the Key Stage 3 strategy is hampering us even more and it's nonsense. Horrible. (Sheila)

Sheila appears to believe that there are circumstances beyond her control which inhibit her ability to teach in a way she understands to be good practice. The adoption of what might be deemed AfL techniques, strategies or procedures does not sufficiently seem to aid her in creating the classroom culture she claims to want. Moreover, it would appear that in this sense Sheila enjoys less of a symbiotic relationship, than Angela, between the underlying principles of formative assessment and how she views the process of learning and the learner. Formative practices map onto Sheila's lessons as procedures, which can be adopted to change the behaviour of pupils, as an aid towards their greater independence, only and if they are ready or able to take them on board.

The spirit and the letter of AfL

The key to the research, however, was what these principles of AfL looked like in the classroom and so we will return now to the videos which were taken as part of the project. As we have already said, the three factors from the school level questionnaire were used in a semi-structured analysis of these videos – Making Learning Explicit, Promoting Learning Autonomy and Performance Orientation.

We found that, having watched the 27 lessons at least three times, as part of a group and then individually, two clear categories of AfL emerged, that of the spirit and the letter of formative assessment. The spirit is characterized as Dewey's 'high organization based on ideas', where the underpinning principle is pupil autonomy. This is in contrast to those lessons where only the procedures or letter of AfL, seem in place.

These two headings under which we characterized AfL have a colloquial resonance, which echo something of the differences we are trying to capture. In colloquial terms, the expression – adhering to the spirit, rather than the letter – implies an underlying principle, which does not allow a simple application of rigid procedure. Sticking to the letter of a particular rule is likely to lose the underlying spirit it was intended to embody. Any crude binary coding is, however, unlikely to capture the complexity of the way in which teachers implement changes in their practice. But comparing two types of lessons can give a better understanding of what the spirit of AfL looks like in a lesson.

Discussing a lesson, which captures the spirit of AfL, in conjunction with one that follows the letter helps highlight the way in which lessons can either promote or constrain learner autonomy. The grid below gives a brief outline of the main activities in two such contrasting English lessons, each with a Year 8 class.

Letter	Spirit
Yr 8 Lesson A – Pre 20th C short story (Tracy)	*Yr 8 Lesson B Pre 20th C poem (Angela)*
• Teacher models criteria to be used for peer assessment by asking pupils to correct technical errors in text prepared by teacher • Pupils correct text • Teacher checks answers with whole class • Pupils correct each other's work	• Class draw up list of criteria guided by teacher • Teacher and LSA perform poem • Pupils asked to critique performance • Pupils rehearse performance • Pupils peer assess poems based on criteria • Pupils perform poems based on criteria

It should be noted that both lessons could have been, while not identical, very similar: even though one is designed around talk and the other around writing, one around performance the other written expression, in particular grammar. Tracy could have asked the pupils to consider what was actually said both in her text and the pupils' rather than just examining technical errors. In other words she could have asked them to look at the meaning of what they had written rather than whether they had missed a full stop or failed to put capital letters.

Having said that the lessons do share much in common. Both Tracy and Angela ask pupils to engage with pre-twentieth century texts, a requirement of the National Curriculum in English. In Tracy's lesson pupils were looking at a letter they had written based on a Victorian short story and in Angela's they were asked to consider a dramatic rendition of a nineteenth century poem that they had begun looking at in the previous lesson. Both lessons had the potential for pupils to engage with the question of what makes for quality in a piece of work – an issue which is difficult in English and hard for pupils to grasp (See Marshall 2004a, 2004b). Significantly both Tracy and Angela adopt procedures of formative assessment as identified by Black and Wiliam (1998a, 1998b) – sharing the criteria with the learner and peer and self-assessment as a means to this end. For these two activities – modeling and peer assessment – are linked. In both lessons the modeling activity at the start of the lesson appears to be designed to help pupils know what to do when they peer assess.

Tracy, however, modeled the criteria for the eventual peer assessment activity by giving pupils a piece of writing which was full of technical errors (i.e. spelling and punctuation). They were asked to correct it on their own while she went around the class monitoring their progress. All these interchanges revolved around notions of correctness and there was little scope for anything other than closed questions. The second activity in Tracy's lesson again centred on the teacher checking whether or not the pupils had found the errors in the text. The feedback involved pupils volunteering where they had found a mistake and correction they had made. Occasionally they missed something in the text and Tracy would go back until a pupil identified the missing error and corrected it. Similarly, on the small number of occasions when a pupil got the answer wrong Tracy would pause, waiting for another pupil to volunteer the right answer. In this exchange the teacher adjudicated questions of correctness with no opportunity for the pupils to extend the narrowly defined scope of the task. Pupils then went on to peer assess each other's work.

Dialogue 1

Angela, on the other hand, modeled the criteria for peer assessment differently. She began the lesson by asking the pupils to draw up a list of criteria for performing a poem. Through the interaction that followed she also developed the pupils' critical vocabulary, as the pupils' contributions were negotiated with the teacher who, through exchange, refined them.

> P: You could speed it up and slow it down
> T: Yes – pace, that's very important in reading [teacher then writes the word 'pace' on the board]

Substituting the word 'pace' is important for in so doing she introduces them to technical vocabulary. It might have been even better if she had told them what she was doing, but it is, nevertheless, significant. Interestingly the Japanese have a useful term for describing such a process – 'neriage', which literally means polishing. In Japan recapitulating the contributions made by pupils is an important part of teachers' classroom practice. It provides an opportunity for teachers to synthesize the contributions made by different pupils, to interject specific vocabulary, and also to refine or re-contextualize ideas.

In another series of interchanges, between the pupils and Angela, it is again the pupils' ideas that are being sought. And, as with the previous dialogue, it is the teacher who tries to understand.

P: It [the performance] was boring.

T: What do you mean boring?

P: There wasn't enough expression in your face when the poem was being read or in the reading.

T: So what could I have done to make it better?

P: You could have looked and sounded more alarmed

T: Like this? [strikes a pose]

P: Not quite

T: More like this? [strikes another pose]

P: Yeah.

The reading by the learning support assistant (LSA) was accompanied by a freeze frame by the teacher (the section selected was one of the most dramatic in the poem). Pupils were invited to comment on both the reading and the freeze frame and in so doing drew not just on the criteria but also on their interpretation of the poem. In this way the dual nature of the lesson – developing their understanding of the literature and of speaking and listening was also served.

In this way the locus of control shifts from the teacher to the pupil, although, as Perrenoud suggests, it is the teacher who regulates the learning environment by adjusting the activity 'once it has been initiated' (Perrenoud, 1998). Perrenoud's theory of AfL, or what he calls the regulation of learning, is, again, useful here. For him, as we have seen in looking at Kate's lesson, the nature of the tasks planned for a lesson significantly impacts on the scope and potential of subsequent interaction and feedback between pupil and teacher as the lesson progresses. Again, Perrenoud differentiates between those sequences of lessons which he calls 'traditional', which merely allow for the remediation of narrowly prescribed concepts at the end of the sequence of work, and those lessons where the tasks are not 'imposed on the pupils but [adjusted] once they have been initiated' (Perrenoud, 1998, p. 88) in order to take the learning forward.

These three tasks in Angela's lesson – the creation of the criteria, the performance of the poem and the application of the criteria to Angela's and the LSA's performance – governed both the pupils' thinking about what was needed when they acted out the poem themselves and the peer assessment of those performances.

High organization based on ideas

Two crucial but subtle elements, then, differentiate Angela and Tracy's lessons – the potential scope of the tasks and the opportunities these afforded for current and future pupil independence. Although it is hard to separate out the various aspects of the lessons, as they overlap, it is possible to use the factor headings – Making Learning Explicit, Promoting Learner Autonomy and Performance Orientation – taken from the staff questionnaire as a way of organizing the analysis.

If we start with Making Learning Explicit: to begin with the scope of the task in Tracy's lesson was considerably more restricted in helping pupils understand what quality might look like, focusing instead on those things which were simply right and wrong. Pupils in Angela's lesson, on the other hand, engaged both in technical considerations, such as clarity and accuracy, as well as the higher order, interpretive concepts of meaning and effect. In addition, the modelling of what was required in Angela's lesson ensured that pupils went beyond an imitation of that model because it challenged them to think about the variety of ways they might enact their interpretation of the poem.

The sequence of activities guided the pupils in Angela's lesson towards being independent or autonomous learners, (the second of our factor headings) because the tasks, including encouraging the pupils to create their own criteria, helped them to think for themselves about what might be needed to capture the meaning of the poem in performance. In so doing they are very like what Pete and Morag say in the interviews about peer assessment. In Tracy's lesson, however, the AfL procedures, alone, were insufficient to lead to this key beneficial outcome of Angela's lesson.

Pupils in Angela's lesson, therefore, also began to engage in the more complex issues of any performance be it verbal or written. That is the pupils were asked to explore the relationship between the meaning of a product and the way in which that meaning is expressed; between form and content. This leads us to the final element of Performance Orientation. Crucially Angela always described the tasks as opportunities for the pupils to improve their performance.

In this way the activities had an open, fluid feel which corresponded with the notion of promoting pupil autonomy; it reinforced a sense of holistic and limitless progress whereby assessment is always seen as a tool for future rather than past performance. In the main this was done by creating tasks designed to enable children to enter the subject community 'guild' (see Sadler, 1989). Performance in Tracy's lesson, by contrast, comprised a finite act, conforming to a fixed, identifiable, measurable notion of correctness in which issues of quality went undiscussed.

Dialogue 2

The nature of the tasks also contributes to the quality and type of dialogue that occurs within the lesson, as we will see from the lesson below. The outline below, in table 5.1, gives a representative sample of the type of dialogue that occurred in one of Sheila's lessons. It is a GCSE lesson on a set text, *An Inspector Calls*, and if we compare this lesson, with for example, Kate's from the last chapter, we will again see the difference between the spirit and the letter of AfL.

Table 5.1 A GCSE lesson

Letter
Yr 10 lesson – An Inspector Calls (Shiela)
• T: Objective for today in form of key question' *This written on board*   T: How are we encouraged to empathize with the characters in their situation'   LSA: What are the key words in this question [*selects pupils as it's a 'hands down class – an AfL technique*]   P: Empathise   LSA: Yes next   P: Situation   LSA: 'C[pupils name] any other key words [*extensive wait*] Miss is pointing to it

P: How

T: Why am I pointing to it. What kind of word is it?

P: A question

T: It is a command word

• *Pupils given 3 minutes in groups to work out the answer to the question teacher speaks to one group*

T: Ok specifically look at two things we always look at?

P: What they say and what they do?

T: Is there a lot of what they do?

P: No

T: So?

P – How they say

• *Whole class feedback on group work [hands down technique made explicit]*

T: Ok I would like you to explain what you have to do?

P: *Pupil doesn't respond*

T: S could you develop that?

S: How

T: What they say and how they say it . . .

T: Can you help me N on showing behaviour is spontaneous' *[pupil replies but Sheila tells him he is mumbling] N repeats his answer answer which his still indistinct*

T: Anything else? The rest of you need to listen at the because while N is helping me at the moment this could move around the room.

3 more pupils respond

T: Good the ideas are developing

Fourth pupil responds

P: It has to be spontaneous because they don't know what's happened before.

Sheila repeats this response and then asks the class if they agree. Most appear to nod in assent She then says

T: Are you agreeing with me because its easier or because you do?

Again there is general assent and they move onto the next task outlined below

• *Sheila gives the pupils the group task of writing a monologue of one of the characters. Photocopies of one done yesterday are handed out as a model*

• *Teacher and LSA go around the groups (Sample of dialogue below)*

(Continued)

Table 5.1 (Cont'd)

Letter
T: The sooner you get below the surface the sooner you'll understand why he behaves as he does T: You don't have to use this format but I think it's fun T: No, no, no, you've got to write it as if Mr Birling [a character in the play] is saying it, as if the speech is from him T: You can use the information on the sheet just change the style T: I want one version. I want you to work together to share your ideas • *Pupils asked to set target for lesson in terms of the key question and the extent to which they have completed the task in their groups*

In Sheila's English lesson the learning is made explicit through instruction, which is then teased out through a series of closed questions. The sequence of activities themselves are less of a useful aid in making the learning explicit. This is because there is a disjunction between the initial objective of the learning outcome – phrased as a question – and the subsequent activity – writing a monologue as one of the characters. Perhaps for this reason the instructional tenor of the exchanges continues beyond the opening phase of the lesson and into the group activity. Despite the apparent idea for group work to foster an, 'exchange of ideas' there is little discussion of ideas in the lesson at all. That which does occur, for example around the nature of spontaneity, appears to be perceived on the pupils' part as leading to a right answer – they all agree with the teacher when she repeats a pupil's response. She does challenge this response on their part 'Are you agreeing with me because it's easier or because you do?' But the way in which she appropriates the pupil's answer to become 'agreeing with me' suggests that the pupils' reading of this whole exchange as moving to a point when one of them hits what is in the teacher's head. And this is so, perhaps, despite the teacher's rhetoric of 'Good the ideas are developing'. In this sense the exchange is convergent rather than divergent to use Torrance and Pryor's model (1998).

Moreover, the above exchange has been immediately preceded, and so framed, by a sequence which is closed and again instructional in nature – 'Explain what you have to do'. The development of the answer to this question also moves to a right answer, or rather a correct formula, as a very similar formula has been given earlier on in the lesson. In addition, references to the techniques of questioning (see Black et al, 2003, James et al. 2007) such as hands down, wait time and 'this could move around the room' are foregrounded in the classroom dialogue. But, in this instance, they appear more as surface features of the lesson, providing pupils with only a limited opportunity to extend and deepen their grasp of the central activity of the lesson – an understanding of the characteristics of a good monologue.

The activities in Sheila's lessons are, however, tightly framed in that all pupils engage in the same task and within the same time constraints. Essay questions appear to be predetermined by exam syllabi, but the nature of this kind of tight framing was evident in all the lessons, not just the exam classes, we observed. In this way Sheila's lesson, or indeed in any of the 27 lessons we watched, appeared to provide much scope for genuine open endedness or pupil choice. So, in that sense, pupil autonomy could only be expressed in limited ways, within the tasks set.

Nevertheless the type of activities in Sheila's class, in some ways, do not even express pupil autonomy in a limited way. Her lesson has a more frag-mented feel, because one activity does not arise naturally out of the previous one, as say, in Angela's lesson. And, perhaps because of this, the exchanges she is involved in mean that much of the dialogue revolves around, simply, the clarification of the task. This in turn makes the pupils more dependent on the judgment of the teacher and the recitation of preset formulae – 'What they say and what they do' – and less on their own understanding.

It should be said though, that as with the Angela's Year 8 lesson mentioned earlier, the emphasis is on what can be done to improve performance rather than viewing performance in any way as fixed or as a finite event. Again the tasks in Angela and Kate's lessons, from KMOFAP, build on guild knowledge in the pupils (see Sadler, 1989).

Questioning does play a role within this enterprise, as questions appear intended both to take the pupils' thinking further through follow up demands for clarification, and, as above, tend to require pupils to refine their answer in terms of the central aim – understanding what constitutes quality or a good answer. The iteration between individual responses on notions of quality, class discussion and peer assessment reinforce the notion of quality as a communal property to be understood rather than an unitary concept to be acquired (Sfard, 1998) Again, this is typical of those lessons which seemed to capture more of the spirit of AfL, expressed as 'high organisation based on ideas', in particular those that attempt to promote learner autonomy.

Conclusion

Both the observation and interview data were collected at the midpoint of the project. They paint a picture of only a few teachers capturing, through AfL practices, what the promise of the Trojan Horse offers – the promotion of learner autonomy. One possible explanation is that the beliefs teachers hold about learning impact on the way they apply AfL in the classroom. This may help us understand why change in classroom practice is so hard to achieve in general (Fullan, 2001) and what Kennedy (1999) calls 'the problem of enactment'. The evidence of this project suggests that teachers need to engage in debates about learning, as well act on practical advice, to bring about change.

It seems, also, that the beliefs of some teachers map more readily onto what we have called the spirit of AfL. This is partly because they value pupil autonomy and see it as a key goal of their teaching, but it also has something to do with how they see the classroom as a site of their own learning. Each of the teachers whose practice we viewed as illustrating the spirit of AfL had an essentially progressive rather than a fixed view of what went on in any given lesson. Neither circumstance nor the disposition of pupils were beyond change. Indeed these provided a challenge to be reflected upon and overcome. Such an attitude gives these teachers a far greater sense of agency than those who tended to see constraints in the school culture, the examination system or the ability of the pupils.

Finally, it appears that the four original headings, under which AfL practice was conceived – questioning, feedback, sharing criteria and self-assessment – need revision. What we have called the spirit of AfL is instantiated in the way teachers conceptualize and sequence the tasks undertaken by pupils in the lesson. The nature of these tasks affects all subsequent interactions within the class. Moreover, these tasks tend to create an environment in which learning is socially constructed. In other words AfL demands 'high organization based on ideas' if it is going to help pupils become independent learners.

All these are important, then, in establishing AfL in the classroom. AfL is not the sole preserve of English teachers. Some English teachers adopt the letter rather than the spirit of AfL, as the examples of Sheila and Tracy demonstrate. But done well it speaks not only to Dewey's 'high organization based on ideas' but also his sense of English as an art. For Dewey, as we have seen, 'To be truly artistic, a work must be aesthetic – that is framed for enjoyed receptive perception' (Dewey, 2005, p. 49). And that, in some respects, is what these teachers in KMOFAP and LHTL achieved. They saw their lessons as an artefact but also knew that the artefact had to be both received and enjoyed by its participants – the pupils. Like an artist these teachers constantly changed, examined the lesson, the artefact, through the eyes of the people it was for, the pupils. If it did not go well, or there appeared a fault, they did not blame the pupils but the lesson. Teaching English, then is an art.

What we will go on to look at in the next chapter is a project which sought to combine both the formative and summative aspects of teaching in a 100 per cent course-based assessment.

6 A Return to Portfolios and the King's Oxfordshire Summative Assessment Project

The King's Oxfordshire Summative Assessment Project (KOSAP) was developed to find a course-based alternative to the summative assessment carried out in England for 14-year-olds – the key stage 3 test. What is interesting about the project is that it started life as a DfES funded project. It appeared that the DfES were interested to see if a portfolio style assessment might work at KS3. In this respect, it was not unlike the trials done on coursework in the 50s and 60s by LATE and the JMB. Although they promised nothing they funded KOSAP for the first 18 months, starting in 2003. They did not, however, continue to fund it and so for the final two years the project was funded by the Nuffield Foundation. The eventual decision by the DCSF, however, even though it is non-statutory, to assess pupil performance by APP, is an indication that some form of course-based assessment is possible. As we shall see, though, it lacks the rigour of moderation of KOSAP.

KOSAP was also important because, in effect, it provides discussion among English teachers of what course-based assessment might look like. We have not had an entirely course-based exam since 1994 and so many of the teachers coming into the English teaching profession are products of a system that has had key stage tests and they have never experienced an examination entirely based on coursework at school. This was the case with four out of the six people who took part in the project. Hearing their views on what was 100 per cent coursework was revealing.

Because the KS3 tests were still ongoing throughout the period of the project it was decided to assess the progress of pupils at 13, Year 8. It involved three schools in Oxfordshire who were picked because they were seen as having good formative practice in their classrooms. The project itself, however, dealt largely with summative assessment – what a pupil was to get at the end of Year 8. Two subjects were involved – maths and English, but for the purposes of this book we will look only at the English.

Over the course of the first year the English teachers who were involved in the project came up with a portfolio of what they thought should be assessed by the end of Year 8, which differed little from that which they generally assessed at the end of the year any way. All three schools operated some kind of portfolio of work as part of their ongoing assessment process. What differed was that now that portfolio was to be formerly assessed. Previously all three schools had just had some kind of ad hoc arrangement whereby individual teachers gave levels of achievement, but the portfolio was never formally moderated by other people in the department and most certainly not between schools.

This changed. Although the content did not change substantially, they added speaking and listening to what was to be assessed and the standards were more rigorously applied, in that the portfolios were now to be moderated across the department and between schools. The portfolio they decided on included three each of reading, writing and speaking and listening assignments but they overlapped, so that there was an assignment where reading and writing were assessed together and one where reading and speaking and listening were jointly marked.

Three interviews were also carried out with the participating teachers. In one of the schools, one teacher came late to the process and so was only interviewed twice. In all other schools both teachers were part of the project throughout the three and a half years. The transcripts of interviews and of discussions were analysed, using a coding scheme partially derived from theory and partially grounded in the data (Glaser and Strauss, 1967). Reliability in the application of agreed codes was cross-checked between pairs of team members. Again Eisner's concept of connoisseurship was used to critically appraise the interviews.

The benefits of coursework

While we will go on and look at some of the difficulties that the teachers encountered in moderating the work, it is first useful to see how they saw English, like the KMOFAP teachers, and how this affected their view of how pupils should be assessed. Rather like those teachers, who, in Chapter 3, so violently disagreed with the exam form of testing at KS3, these teachers also seemed to like course-based assessment. One teacher put it most plainly. 'I mean I would be completely in support of having a kind of coursework approach to KS3' (EB1). Her reasons are plain. 'It's very artificial in an exam to ask the students to respond creatively to a very, very dry stimulus' (EB1). Another comments, 'It's all about creating, releasing creativity of the moment' (KSE3).

Both these remarks come out of a belief in what it means to be good at English. Katrina, the second to comment on the tests, thinks that to be good at English means that you have 'insight' but not particularly across the three attainment targets. So in reading she says, 'Insight and a second a kind of analysis, a kind of sharpness and precision of analysis, of language' adding,

> insight is also important. They can't become of this sort of mechanical analysis. It's got to be married up to some sort of crisp understanding . . . and the most sophisticated readers will understand what kind of message or a meaning behind, some sort of sense of authorial tension. (KSE3)

'In writing' she comments, 'there will be a kind of adventurousness to it. Often imaginative writers subvert conventions or subvert questions. They'll be technically accurate though not necessarily superb' (KSE3). Others talk of 'flair' and 'confidence'.

What is evident from these observations is that none of the teachers viewed English as a set of communication skills but rather saw English as an art. This would not matter if English, as we have seen, were a tidy subject with a clear sense of parameters in which the items, which were to be assessed, were clearly identifiable and quantifiable, but they are not. Some of the teachers even saw that they emphasized one quality, not so much at the expense of, but certainly more than another. Katrina, for example, says, 'I know that in reading I've privileged precision in analysis and possibly disproportionally' (KS3).

Yet the one thing on which these English teachers were agreed is that English should not be atomized into a tick list of criteria, which are easily assessable. 'I don't mind marking. It's when you're marking in a very narrow way, where you're not allowed to make assumptions that deadens' (KSE1) says Katrina. What is interesting is she believes that not to make 'assumptions' about a piece a child has written 'deadens' the whole process. To mark, you read into what is written; you assume certain patterns. Not to do this narrows and eventually 'deadens' the marking. This can make marking 'Tricky' according to Natasha.

> There is a difference between what you can actually . . . you could go through and underline all the connectives and say 'yes' they are using those well and they are solid or they mark out an argument and then insight again. It's not as tangible as that and that is what makes marking the hard part. You can read something and demonstrate insight . . . [you] go through and find where the writer has created a sense of atmosphere. It's tricky. It's not like you go through and find all the verbs. So there is a difference. (NC1)

Even those qualities which she thinks are a bit more 'solid' have a nebulous or vague quality. For instance she comments that a good argument is 'mark[ed] out' but in another essay the argument may just emerge and with sufficient 'insight' this might be a better way of approaching it. Or atmosphere – clearly this can't simply be judged by counting the verbs. Some other criteria will have to be used.

Natasha feels, therefore, that there is a difference between the success criteria, for example, of using 'connectives' and one for 'insight'. One has 'tangible' qualities, the other is open to interpretation. Nevertheless 'insight' is a word she uses in class.

> We always look at the mark scheme and then again that doesn't really give much of an idea of what the word actually means . . . I'd like to think I try, I do try and model it in a way. You know we will have a discussion . . . and I will say 'stop you have just shown me that'. It's more of a kind of them doing it and then me saying 'well you may not realise it that that was what you were doing'. (NC1)

'Insight' is something which can be used when talking, writing or even when commenting on something a child has read. Whether or not a child has shown insight, however, is open to debate and this makes making such a decision 'tricky'. It makes the subjective choices that a teacher can make more dominant than perhaps they should be.

Construct referencing and guild knowledge

Yet there is evidence, as we have seen, that despite the apparent subjectivity of response teachers internalize what a level or grade looks like. Dylan Wiliam's (1998) 'construct referencing' (19) and Royce Sadler's 'guild knowledge' (1989) seemed to apply to this set of teachers too. Despite the possible ambiguity of arriving at a level, over what 'insight' might mean, for example, the disagreements at the KOSAP moderation meetings were minor. The teachers seemed to have internalized what a particular level looked like.

The KOSAP project held two moderation meetings – one half way through the project and one at the end. The first was seen, in a way, as a trial run for the second. In both, however, the moderation of the speaking and listening element was problematic, but of this there will be further discussion. In the first meeting the class teacher marked the portfolios and then they were sent to the other two schools for moderation. In the second meeting the work had been marked and levelled by the individual teacher. A sample was then blind marked by rest of the department and given a level. These portfolios were sent to the other two participating schools, who again blind marked them, and gave them a level as well. Altogether there were nine portfolios to assess, each school assessing three from their own school and six from the two others.

In both sessions a school had put in a folder that was seen as particularly problematic and on each occasion it provoked considerable debate. What was interesting was that whichever the school was, they added a great deal of background information that you would not normally have when receiving a folder without a grade. In the first instance the child had had a number of supply teachers and in the second a weak teacher and then a much better one. In both cases they were particularly difficult to assess because the work varied in quality so much. In the end it was decided that despite the temptation to assess the potential of the children one could only assess what was there. At this point it became easier to give a level. The fact that one could only assess the evidence that was there, however, did provoke much controversy.

What is interesting is that the teachers were able to share with their pupils some sense of 'guild knowledge' in the process of writing the assignments and they did it predominantly through peer assessment – assessing others' work. Karen, for example, says that she uses 'peer assessment' all the time, as does Katrina

> I also do quite a lot of peer and self-assessment . . . what's been really interesting is watching how the processes between peer and self-assessment has actually will find their sensibilities about what a particular skill actually constitutes. So, the beginning we were very mechanical and quite tick boxy about, you know, use of variety sentences and sort of count up . . . And now they, they, they've kind of internalised it. (KSE3)

So although she started with an approach that could be called 'quite tick boxy' she has ended up with a class who have 'internalised' the process. She goes on to explain it further:

> I guess what, I would hope what they're burning up is good knowledge and I guess in the case of some students that has happened. It has also legitimised their own sense of what quality is because I've sometimes said, you know, it might not fit in a box, why is this good or why is that bad, and I think (Pause) to me it works both ways round when you get assessed and then that piece of work gets assessed with strengths and weaknesses, in terms of the whole process it assesses really their ability to understand what quality is. (KSE3)

The class have gained 'good knowledge' of 'quality' that cannot be expressed in a tick box. They have moved from counting the variety of sentences to recognizing that 'quality' is something more and this is a good thing. Although, immediately afterwards, Katrina adds, 'their understanding of the particular concept like writing, sentence structure and analysis of language' (KSE3) she does so within the overall context of quality work, which is a very vague, non-specific term. Even 'analysis of language' or sentence structure become less definable because they are predicated by 'quality' and the 'concept' of writing. Writing in this sense has become more of an abstract, more of a 'concept' that can be seen in many ways. In this sense she requires that her class make artistic judgements.

   This is very like Eisner's view on art, which in a way is the antithesis of the tick box approach, or what Dewey disparagingly calls 'ledger entries' (2005, p. 44). For Eisner, as we have seen, art was about, 'Judgement in the absence of rules. Indeed, if there were rules for making such choices, judgement would not be necessary' (Eisner, 2002, p. 77). He goes on to write, 'Work in the arts, unlike many other rule-governed forms of performance, always leave the door open to choice, and choice in this domain depends upon a sense of rightness' (ibid., p. 77). His notion of judgement and, too, the sense of rightness depend upon an appreciation of the aesthetic and of artistry. In so doing, then, the pupils in Katrina's class have developed a 'guild knowledge' of artistry and the aesthetic.

It is a view echoed in Natasha's responses also. Although in her first interview she still has some affinity to a check list of criteria, 'I kind of see it in terms of boxes they are ticking and they are ticking the high boxes because they have got those words like insight and layers of meaning' (NC1), by her second interview she remarks that those criteria need to be more openly applied.

> We are putting more of an emphasis on these sort of independent learning . . . being more creative, not necessarily giving them the success criteria – even the 'must, could, should' . . . I think . . . that's also influenced our, our GCSE thinking as well because giving them a lot of scope . . . Creating the scope so you know, having open ended success criteria, getting them to design the task success criteria themselves . . . I think that when we first started using them [must, could, should] it was like 'brilliant this is great' because it gets them to make independent choices themselves about what they are going to do. You know they want to do the shoulds and the coulds . . . but at the same time it's still quite fixed. So the next step is to think about how can we open up those criteria. (NC2)

And this makes her doubt the efficacy of the tick box. 'There is a danger in that you approach it like that. "Oh they've done that, they put a paragraph in . . . they've done something interesting with verbs" so you start thinking in more of a tick box way' (NC2). Like Katrina she has developed a sense of what 'guild knowledge' might be and has communicated this to her pupils all be it in an amorphous kind of way. What it means to have insight, for example, can no longer be ticked off. How the pupils use verbs has to be dependent on some form of what Eisner calls 'judgement'. The criteria have to be 'opened up' so that there is the element of 'choice' (ibid.).

In this way the formative process informs that summative product, particularly through peer assessment. Natasha, like Katrina, has established the same kind of critical readings of assignments through pupils marking each other's work, 'They are marking each others [drafts]' (NC2). So pupils have begun to acquire a sense of what a 'construct' of a particular level or grade looks like through the act of reading each other's work in a critical capacity, and, in so doing, begun to extend their aesthetic understanding. As Liz put it: 'Ongoing assessment means that everything is valued. I think it would mean a richer curriculum because I think preparing for exams is reductive' (EB2).

The dilemmas of coursework

Yet if pupils and teachers alike had gained an idea of the aesthetic quality of a piece of work, and developed a sense of what the 'construct' of a particular level looked like, this is did not mean that the portfolio that the teachers had originally designed was without problems. One central dilemma was that they had attempted to assess both reading and writing together in one assignment. On the face of it this should not have been problematic. It is done as part of GCSE coursework and reading is generally assessed through the writing process. But for Karen it was 'Just impossible to do' adding 'I don't see how you can meaningfully assess both at the same time in terms of a written piece of work' (K3).

Combinations of reading and writing

This highlighted, for two of the teachers from the same school, the way in which their assessment of reading had became problematic. Daniel commented:

> It really made us think about how we assess reading across KS3 and how we rely on essays. The kind of lit crit, analytical outcome, which it's very hard to mark for reading . . . And it's really difficult to separate out the writing from the . . . in the end we were just giving a kind of vague impression mark, which was overly influenced by their ability to write . . . we were assess writing much more than we were assessing reading . . . the writing was taking over. (DG2)

While Liz observed, 'A huge part of our teaching ends up being about how to teach writing essays, not teaching a sophisticated reading response'. She added,

> I think the effect will be that teachers will be able to comment much more widely on students working in English. So I feel like the focus in the past has largely been on writing and I think that the result of this project would be they would comment on their reading skills and on their speaking and listening. I think it will mean a much, you know, a much richer report. (EB2)

The conflation of reading and writing has for both these individuals become an issue yet the problem is that you cannot assess reading on its own. It is either assessed through writing or speaking and listening. In fact part of the problem with both the GCSEs and the KS3 tests was felt to be that there was too much assessment of reading albeit in written form. The KS3 tests in particular had two reading type assignments – a comprehension activity and Shakespeare – and only one for writing – the short and long writing tasks. It was also decided in 2002 that the Shakespeare paper, which had been assessed for reading and writing would only be assessed for reading.

In a way this is the conclusion that Daniel comes to himself, that pieces of work should not be dually tested, that they should either be tested for reading or writing, even though the test of reading will be done in written form. In his final interview he comments,

> I don't think it's difficult to do a piece of writing based on a piece of reading but I think the outcome makes it very difficult to assess two things simultaneously because they so kind of blur into each other. But it's and it's I think its very easy for teacher to end up assessing writing (pause) and call it a reading assessment and it isn't really. (DG3)

What is interesting is that he has come to the conclusion that it is perfectly possible to write about what you have read just that you should not assess for both in the same piece of work. Marking for writing as well as reading can confuse the teacher: the components 'blur into each other'. He does not reduce the components still further, however. In fact later on in the interview he remarks, 'I think two pieces of reading, two pieces of writing assessment is enough. Whereas I think we were looking for three and I think that's probably too many' (DG3) Far from wanting very distinct items to assess reading, it can all be done in 'two pieces'.

None of them, however, talked about assessing the writing of poetry. It is not mentioned by any of the teachers in any of their interviews. Although they did write poetry, in LW, for example, they wrote ballads, the idea of having poetry as an assessable part of the portfolios seems not to have occurred. It is possible that they believed it too hard to assess. This demonstrates one of the difficulties with portfolio assessment – a kind of conservatism. You get pupils to do what you know you can assess and in this way it resembles part of the problem with exams. You test what you can in the time. While the range of work that it is possible to complete in a portfolio is far greater, and it does not stop you completing writing poetry, for instance, it may prevent you from counting it in the final grading. This in many ways echoes the Ofsted report on poetry teaching which noted that teachers did not count it in formal assessments (Ofsted, 2007)

Reading and speaking and listening combined

But to return, again, to that which they did want assessing, the teachers also wanted reading to be assessed, however, through speaking and listening. This again caused an interesting debate for the same two teachers. Another school had set up a system of peer assessed group work which LW adopted. Liz prepared a grid based on Natasha's resources starting with simple questions and working towards the more difficult, 'and each group had to sort of, well group analysis of each group member' (EB2). For Natasha the activity was very successful but for Liz there were problems, namely, how you got round a group of 30 pupils. Although she thought that the groups which she did hear showed good discernment,

> They really went for it in their groups. I was really, really pleased with their response. I heard one group at the end really tussling over one student had shown a particular skill or not, which I thought was really positive. Obviously the difficulty then is when assessing them and say I've only assessed six students in about half a lesson . . . I don't think it's possible for the teacher. (Liz, EB2)

It also caused problems for Katrina, who while she was going to keep the speaking and listening tasks, she needed to 'get them better set up' (KS3). The aim was to have small groups working together on a whole text that they had studied, and what she should have done, she felt, was to keep an ongoing running record on how they performed as groups, completed by the students themselves. This was how she believed Natasha operated.

> But I didn't use that as part of my assessment. I think I just disconnected the two things. But looking at the whole process from the assessment of the task to the final performance and evaluation – that would have been more helpful to me than thinking at which point shall I assess this. Because then I ended up with a kind of unsatisfactory mismatch of marks. (KSE3)

What is interesting about both Liz and Katrina is that they say once they have sorted out some of the problems in the way in which they set the task up they will have no difficulty in assessing reading through this type of speaking and listening activity. Again it is fairly reliant on the pupils themselves having some understanding of how they are assessing themselves. In fact according to Liz, 'Natasha says that it is and that they actually do it instead of [written] coursework at GSCE' (EB2).

This was not universally the case, though. Speaking and listening activities caused more difficulties than anything else. Part of the problem was that although talk in the classroom was vital in stimulating ideas it was difficult to capture and harder still to moderate. To begin with it was ephemeral unless taped. Two activities were taped as part of the moderating process – one was a group activity on poetry, the other was a courtroom drama.

The poetry activity was hard to level because there was insufficient dialogue from each of the pupils and little opportunity for cross discussion. They were given a ballad and had to put it some kind of order. Pupils tended to focus on the text and just shuffle the bits of paper around so that while it may have been a good classroom activity there was insufficient talk for a assessing speaking and listening. Part of the difficulty with the courtroom drama was that, almost inevitably, not everybody had an extensive speaking part. Someone may have been good at speaking and listening but only spoke a little and was therefore difficult to assess.

There was another problem though. It was felt that the level descriptors were not specific enough to enable assessment at KS3. The GSCE criteria were much more explicit. If the pupils were graded according to these criteria then the teachers moderating found it on one level a much easier task to do. Yet in another way, it proved quite difficult because it meant that 13-year-old pupils were awarded high grades in terms of GCSE. One teacher, in particular, found this quite hard to do. It meant, in effect, that a 12-year-old was given the equivalent of a grade 'A' or 'B' at GCSE. Others found that less difficult.

For Katrina the problem was not that the level descriptors were vague and the GCSE precise it was rather that the level descriptors were 'incoherent'. They did not 'represent something that to an English teacher looks like a continuum' (KSE3). This problem extended beyond speaking and listening. She goes on to say,

> You get these weird anomalies saying suddenly in level 7, you get this reference to handwriting. And you think like 'oh great I've sort of taken that for granted and now and now I am worried about handwriting'. And so you think it's the discontinuity which bothers me more than the lack of precision because a lack of absolute precision is kind of what you'd expect from level criteria representing English. (ibid.)

And concludes, 'Sometimes it surprises me English teachers are so in favour of this amount of precision' (ibid.). Her solution, if it was one, was to look to the way GCSE coursework solved the problem:

> If we look at the main criteria for GCSE it's more detailed. But if they're a little bit open to the charge of being imprecise then what they do have is quite good task specific criteria . . . task criteria for original writing, or criteria for a literary critical essay. And that, that might be the balance. There's a real balance between you know representing the kind of continual English skills, which is necessarily a bit imprecise I think, versus giving people real stability and security. (KSE3)

The criteria she is looking for is not part of the general criteria that are used to award pupils levels or grades but task specific. She imagines that while there still be a general, for example, level 5 descriptor, there might also be a more specific one, for instance, on creative writing. She allows for the fact, however, that the criterion for English is necessarily 'imprecise'. In so doing she agrees with Sadler's conclusion that all written descriptions of criteria can be seen as woolly (Sadler, 2009).

Assessing Pupils' Progress

What she is violently opposed to are 'those horrendous APP tasks', which she would like to 'abolish', presumably because they are over precise. QCDA, along with the National Strategies, would, however, beg to differ. We have already looked in Chapter 3 at the way APP was introduced and how for now at least they are to replace the Sats instead of a system like the one in Wales or indeed KOSAP, which moderated work both within and between schools. We have seen that the APP tasks were introduced by the QCDA as a tool for AfL, although it is possible that schools will use them summatively, as we shall see.

For now, it is worth looking at APP in some detail. This is because, in many respects, Assessing Pupils' Progress, represents the manner in which many strategies are changed then adopted, by governments. The literacy hour might be another. We look at it, then, as yet another example of government strategy, rather than looking at APP in and of itself. What becomes evident is that they want to separate out English into parts rather than assess the whole.

The rubric of Assessing Pupils' Progress was first piloted, as we have said, in 2005. At the launch of *Playback*, the conclusion of the *English 21* consultation, a teacher from the north of England described how her school had used them.

They were introduced to members of the KOSAP team in the summer of that year and were finally published at the end of 2006. In October 2008, they were revised to include statements for each level of the national curriculum. At the moment these are for reading and writing, speaking and listening are still be worked on.

Many schools did not take that much notice of the APPs as they have been non-statutory. It now seems, however, that all schools will have to pay attention to them because they are to replace the KS3 tests. In this respect they, too, are a course-based assessment, which is what the teacher from the north of England praised in her discussion of how they had gone when she introduced them to her school. The disadvantage that she might have had is that the coursework was to be followed by Sats, rather as the KOSAP teachers had. Now, however, there are no Sats and the APP is, at present, the only form of assessment.

In a document called *Assessing Pupils' Progress: Assessment at the heart of learning* the QCA write,

> APP is the new structured approach to teacher assessment, developed by QCA in partnership with the National Strategies, which equips teachers to make judgements on pupils' progress. It helps teachers to fine-tune their understanding of learners' needs and to tailor their planning and teaching accordingly, by enabling them to:
>
> - use diagnostic information about pupils' strengths and weaknesses to improve teaching, learning and pupils' progress,
> - make reliable judgements related to national standards drawing on a wide range of evidence,
> - track pupils' progress. (QCA, 2009, p. 3)

APP, then, is intended to be a document that promotes formative assessment. It says that it is 'diagnostic', based on the 'evidence' of what a pupil has done that will improve 'teaching, learning and pupils' progress'. Yet there is something in language that goes against the artiness that the KOSAP had acquired when talking of how they assessed pupils' work.

To begin the document speaks of how it 'equips teachers to make judgements'. It is the word equip that marks this document out as having a slightly more technical feel. Certainly teachers are to make judgements but this is not in the Eisner sense, they are to be equipped to 'fine-tune' their understanding from a 'structured approach'. Although fine-tuning could have musical implications, in this document it seems more mechanical, like something you would do to a car to make it run better. The word 'structured' adds to this slightly mechanistic feel. And while the word 'diagnostic' is a commonly used assessment term it is linked to the word 'information', which implies that there is a problem which can be solved rather than something which can be developed in a variety of ways. It reads negatively rather than positively and again is technisist in approach. The implication is that children are machine like, the teacher the mechanic. Use the APP guidelines and we will be able to 'fine-tune' our interventions so that we can 'track pupils' progress'. Even the word track, in this context, has mechanical connotations: pupils leave a trail which can be followed a narrowed down.

Nevertheless, APPs are course based. What is more the QCA admit that they have to depend on teacher or 'professional judgement' and interpretation to arrive at a specific level:

> Using the assessment criteria inevitably involves a degree of interpretation and professional judgement. Standards files help ensure that judgements made by teachers are consistent and aligned with national standards. (ibid., p. 5)

But they do not ask for standardization meetings to ensure that the assessment is done rigorously, consistently and across schools. In this they are rejecting both the Welsh model and the model for GCSE. They rely first and foremost on the descriptors themselves, the 'standards files', to ensure that teachers make decisions that are 'aligned' with 'national standards'. The word 'aligned' is more of a mathematical term, which belies the earlier use of the phrase 'interpretation' which is more artistic in feel. It is as an afterthought they add, 'Regular collaborative assessment and discussion is another important way of ensuring that assessment standards are reliable and consistent' (ibid., p. 5).

The first two 'benefits' of using APPs are again, however, course based. 'It does not require special assessment activities but involves recognizing evidence from the opportunities generated by planned teaching and learning', and, 'It reduces the need to use tests and specific assessment tasks to make assessment judgements by taking into account a far wider range of evidence. This gives a clearer and more accurate picture of learners achievements and progress' (ibid., p. 6). Although both these benefits have a slightly bureaucratic air with 'planned teaching and learning' and 'a clearer and more accurate picture of learners achievements and progress' they both talk of the need for less testing or 'special assessment activities'. It recognizes the importance of what they do on a day-to-day basis.

The purpose of APP is that it is meant to assess pupils formatively. Yet in the terminology it uses it seems to be more summative in its use (see Smith, 2009). When describing how they should be used the QCDA writes: 'Drawing on the evidence they have selected, the teacher then considers each of the subject assessment focuses carefully and highlights where the criteria have been met across the two levels' (QCDA, 2009, p5) and again,

> Once judgements have been made for each of the assessment focuses, the profile of highlighted criteria allows the teacher to make an informed decision about the overall national curriculum level at which the learner is working. The judgement is made in a holistic way, taking account of how independently, consistently, and in what range of contexts learners demonstrate their skills. (ibid., p. 5)

APP writing

In other words the teacher is asked to make a micro summative assessment of where the pupil is at any given time against their national curriculum level. There are eight assessment foci for writing, nine if you count the descriptor for levels 2 and 3. But it is the order in which they are expressed that is interesting. Although they are numbered from 1–8, with the assessment focus on writing 'imaginative, interesting and thoughtful texts' as the first one, they are not placed in that order. The first one listed is AF5 – 'vary sentences for clarity, purpose and effect'. Next are AF6, 3 and 4 before we get to AFI:

> AF6 – write with technical accuracy of syntax and punctuation in phrases, clauses and sentences
> AF3 – organise and present whole texts effectively, sequencing and structuring information, ideas and events
> AF4 – construct paragraphs and use cohesion within and between paragraphs
> AF1 – write imaginative, interesting and thoughtful texts

This is followed by,

> AF2 – produce texts which are appropriate to task, reader and purpose
> AF7 – select appropriate and effective vocabulary
> AF8 – use correct spelling

Handwriting and presentation (only applies to levels 2 and 3 (ibid., p. 2).

It is as if they know that the most important focus is being able to write thoughtfully and imaginatively but before they can state it they have to put in a number of provisos such as varying sentence length and writing with technical accuracy and so on. Even using appropriate vocabulary comes after a list which focuses on the 'technical'.

Under each of these headings are listed what a pupil might do at each level. A level 5 pupil, for example, under the heading 'correct spelling' will, 'Across a range of writing' spell 'grammatical function words, almost all inflected words, most deviational suffixes and prefixes, most context/lexical words'. The list goes on to suggest those words which they are likely to misspell. Under the sub heading 'Likely errors' it writes 'Occasional phonetically plausible spelling of unstressed syllables in context words, double consonant in prefixes' (ibid., p. 2). The assessment foci only start to amalgamate when the pupil reaches level 7 when AF5 and 6 are combined. Here they write,

- a variety of sentence types deployed judiciously across the text to achieve purpose and overall effect, with rare loss of control
- a range of features employed to shape/craft sentences that have individual merit and contribute to overall development of text *eg. embedded phrases and clauses that support succinct explanation; secure control of complex verb forms; antithesis, repetition or balance in sentence structure* (ibid., p. 2)

When one considers that now a level 7 is the equivalent of a GCSE grade C, this seems quite an achievement. Sentences must have 'individual merit', which is hard. And they must 'contribute to overall development' which is again not easy. But it is the words 'judiciously' and 'rare,' that strike one as being particularly difficult and yet they are in some respects an odd choice of words. There is no place for splurging across a page, or imaginative flights of fancy, no room for a burst of inspiration. All must be controlled, judicious.

In fact the word 'imaginative', in these two assessment foci, only appears at level 8 where students 'sentence structure is imaginative, precise and accurate matched to the writer's purpose and intended effect on the reader' (ibid., p. 2). Even then though, it must be 'precise and accurate'. There is no room for bagginess, apparently, in the English national curriculum. For level 8, in effect there are only five as AF3 and 4 are also linked and AF1 and 2. AF7 and 8 are still separate items. In this way the technical aspects of English are reinforced as it is only at the higher levels, when a pupil is meant to have mastered accuracy, that some of the assessment foci are merged. This echoes the literacy framework, which focused on the 'basics' first before moving on to work which was more imaginative.

APP Reading

For reading there are six assessment foci from level 4 onwards, seven if you count the ones for levels 2 and 3;

> AF1 – use a range of strategies, including accurate decoding of text, to read for meaning (only relates to levels 2 and 3)
>
> AF2 – understand, describe, select or retrieve information, events or ideas from texts and use quotation and reference to text
>
> AF3 – deduce, infer or interpret information, events or ideas from texts
>
> AF4 – identify and comment on the structure and organisation of texts, including grammatical and presentational features at text level
>
> AF5 – explain and comment on writers' use of language, including grammatical and literary features at word and sentence level
>
> AF6 – identify and comment on writers' purposes and viewpoints, and the overall effect of the text on the reader
>
> AF7 – relate texts to their social, cultural and historical traditions (National Strategies, 2008, p. 8)

Again, these only merge at level 8 where AF2 and 3 are combined, along with AF4 and 5. What is striking about these assessment foci is that they are very precise in what they want. Far from the Scottish model, which asks pupils to appreciate texts, and divides out reading for information from reading literature and for pleasure, these are very exacting. In fact the word 'appreciate' is only used when a pupil arrives at level 7.

If, for example, a pupil is to receive a level 6, they are expected under AF2, have identified across a range of reading, 'relevant points clearly identified, including summary and synthesis of information from different sources or different places in the same text' (ibid., p. 11) and a 'commentary' which 'incorporates apt textual reference and quotation to support main ideas or argument' (ibid., p. 11). It is the same under AF5, where the pupil has to give 'some detailed information, with appropriate terminology, of how language is used' and show a 'drawing together of comments on how the writer's language choices contribute to the overall effect on the reader' (ibid., p. 11).

While there is nothing objectionable or intrinsically wrong about either assessment focus in and of itself, it is the exacting demands of each focus that cause some concern. If these AFs were to be taught to specifically, the criteria explained to pupils, then there is the possibility that it might produce a very dry reading of a text. Nowhere is mentioned pleasure or enjoyment. All is analytical, at word, sentence and text level, again echoing the literacy strategy, which wanted pupils to study these three aspects of a piece of writing. Again, although it is possible that these assessment foci could be studied formatively, it is much more likely that they will be studied summatively.

Conclusion

KOSAP was an attempt to see if it was possible to assess pupils through some sort of portfolio of work and in the main it was successful. Moderation between and among schools was done successfully though no official study of reliability was completed. Certain aspects of the course would have to be sorted out. Assessing reading and writing might be difficult, though not impossible, and speaking and listening would need work but essentially pupils could be assessed in this way. The potential conservatism of coursework might also be addressed in the teaching of writing poetry. Fears in the press and the government of plagiarism were not an issue for these teachers as all felt they knew the pupils' work well enough to know whether or not they had had excessive help at home or the work was copied.

The biggest difference to the work carried out at KS3 was its validity. To quote Liz's comment once again, 'Ongoing assessment means that everything is valued. I think it would mean a richer curriculum because I think preparing for exams is reductive' (EB2). Bearing this in mind we will now look at how other English speaking countries have considered some form of course-based assessment.

7 Coursework across the World

It would be tedious to trawl the world for international comparisons but it is interesting to note a few exceptions – the Queensland assessment system in Australia, the English Subject Design in New Zealand and the Vermont assessment in the US. At some point all these systems had a system of assessing pupils' work through 100 per cent coursework. All these systems, however, had different means of ensuring the reliability and validity of these portfolios of pupil work and all had different assessment cultures against which to compete. Only New Zealand was operating in a system of national testing arrangements, the other two were state level but still significant. What is also worth considering is that all these examples have either been abandoned altogether or have had state or government interference that has significantly altered what they once were. It also must be said that two of these systems of assessment, in Australia and New Zealand, were the final examinations which pupils undertook before leaving school. In other words they were the ultimate in high stakes testing.

The United States

We are going to begin, however, in the US, home, some would say, of psychometric testing. This is, of course, not true as most countries involve some kind of psychometrics, but in the States they have become very keen on what they call objective testing and this means multiple-choice tests, which are marked by a computer. What is interesting is that pupils in the classroom are almost entirely assessed and graded by their classroom teacher – for this is what assessment to most in the States means. It would seem, therefore, to be an ideal example of teacher assessment and portfolios of pupil work but there is very little research on what goes on between the four walls of that classroom apart from the examples that we will be looking at. There is little evidence, for instance, of moderation between teachers as to the grades they have given. Nevertheless all the pupil's grades are added up at the end of a year and they are given a grade point average. This is curious in a system so dominated by questions accountability that no one ever checks the teachers' grades.

Perhaps this is because, dominating the system are the state tests. Results are published at either a school and, or, state level: the individual does not get his or her grade but the impact of these tests can be quite considerable. One only has to think of series 4 of the cult hit programme *The Wire* to realize that state tests influence, and some would say control, the way people teach. This pressure has increased since the No Child Left Behind legislation introduced in 2001 under the Bush administration where underachieving schools were placed under huge obligation to improve their results, particularly in literacy.

Individual states set their own exams because education is not federally funded. Education is a local issue and often the curriculum of a school is decided at the school board level but since the 60s the state has become more involved, partly because it gives more money and most states now have some form of state exams. In California, for instance, the state has all children from grades 2 to 11 take the Stanford Achievement Test under the Standardized Testing and Reporting Program. This involves pupils from grades 2 to 8 taking tests in reading, writing, spelling and maths and in grades 9 to 11 being examined in reading, writing, maths, science and social studies (Wiliam, 2009). Other states introduced state wide testing; for example Massachusetts did so in 1986 and Texas did so in 1990 under the Texas Assessment of Academic Skills. The tests of reading are almost exclusively done by multiple-choice marked by computer.

Wiliam attributes the reliance of this form of testing on the Scholastic Aptitude Tests or SATs, which are used for university entrance. Unlike European models, which examine what you have already learned, either in A-levels, Highers or some form of Baccalaureate, the SATs are essentially a test of your potential, of your likely skills and intelligence. They really came in to their own in the second half of the twentieth century and are almost entirely based on multiple-choice exams (a test of short answer writing was introduced in 2005). In 1959 a new test was introduced called the American College Testing (ACT) by Lindquist and McCarrell which has gained popularity and now almost as many take this exam alongside the SAT. While claiming to be different it appears to test almost the same as the SAT. In some way ill defined, the SAT has earned the right, in American terms at least, to be thought of as an objective test.

> As the demand to hold schools accountable grew during the final part of the twentieth century, the technology of multiple-choice testing that had been developed for the SAT was easily pressed into service for the assessment of younger children. (ibid., p. 177)

The problem with state testing is that there is no way of comparing one state test with another. As Bolon suggested, when reviewing the development of statewide testing systems, individual states appeared to be in a competition which implied that, 'Our standards are different from yours' (Bolon, cited in Wiliam, 2009). There is, however, a nationwide system of testing organized by the National Centre for Educational Statistics but written by the Education Testing Service. These are completed by a randomized sample of pupils, across the country, at grades 4, 8 and 12 in both public and private sector schools. Called the National Assessment of Educational Progress (NAEP) these tests used to be carried out at four-yearly intervals but with the No Child Left Behind legislation it changed to being two years.

A quick glance at the statistics produced as result of this exercise shows that there is a wide variation between the various test scores of the different states. In their reading tests for example, 8th graders in Louisiana had considerably lower scores than those students in Massachusetts. In 2007, for example, 41 per cent of students in Massachusetts are seen as basic, 39 per cent as proficient and 4 per cent as advanced compared to 45 per cent basic, 18 per cent proficient and 1 per cent advanced in Louisiana. The worst set of results come from the District of Columbia, which has 52 per cent of the students achieving a below basic standard and only 11 per cent achieving proficient and 1 per cent acquiring advanced (IES, 2007a). If we look at the state tests, however, we see that Louisiana, which changed its base line assessments that year, requires that over 80 per cent of all 8th Graders receive basic in English or Math (ibid., 2007b). If then, you were seen as reasonably bright by Louisiana standards you would barely count as average in Massachusetts.

It was into this maelstrom of variation that Vermont chose to make its assessment portfolio-based and not to rely on the tried and tested multiple-choice exams. In 1991 Sarah Warshaur Freedman wrote an article on the forthcoming way in which pupils in grades 4 and 11 in Vermont were going to be assessed in writing English. Called *Evaluating Writing Linking Large Scale Testing and Classroom Assessment* it looked at how students would submit a portfolio of work, which would later be moderated by teachers, for a final State grade in writing. It considered a number of examples of similar types of assessment but the main examples were from the UK – the Primary Learning Record and the NEAB's 100 per cent coursework in GSCE. The reasons for wanting to introduce a portfolio of pupils' work have now become familiar. Quoting a paper by J. C. Mellon written in 1975, on behalf of the National Council of Teachers of English, Freedman cites the claim that answering a written question in exam conditions is an artificial exercise.

> We all know that it is difficult enough to devote half an hour's worth of interest and sustained effort to writing externally imposed topics carrying the promise of teacher approbation and academic marks. But to do so as a flat favour to a stranger would seem to require more generosity and dutiful compliance than many young people can summon up.
>
> . . . Answering multiple-choice questions without a reward in mathematics or science lesson may be one thing. Giving of the self what one must give to produce an effective prose discourse, especially if it is required solely for the purposes of measurement and evaluation, is quite another. (Mellon, cited in Freedman, 1991, p. 34)

The complaint sounds remarkably like those teachers in the UK justifying why they disliked the exam system they faced and why they believed coursework was a more authentic way of assessing somebody's ability in English. What is interesting to note is that Vermont was not adopting the stringent moderation procedures of the NEAB. Freedman's paper went on to analyse how the NEAB managed to ensure that the marking was consistent but the model adopted in Vermont was much less robust. Initially class teachers marked the portfolio and then a sample were marked externally. Later this was changed and a non-class teacher assessed the portfolio but nothing like the rigour of the NEAB was contemplated.

This might have contributed to the unhealthy reports of the reliability of the assessment. Koretz (1998) provided a number of reports on the reliability of this and other portfolio based assessments: the one in Vermont, which formed the predominant core of state based assessment, one in Kentucky, which provided only part of the state exams, a small-scale experiment in Pittsburgh and finally a project organized by the NAEP. In the end Koretz believed that the nature of reliability in the Vermont portfolio work showed little more than chance correlations between markers from different schools. This was damning indeed. In fact the only project that showed any success in reliability was the one in Pittsburgh.

> Its evaluators concluded that the Pittsburgh experience showed that 'contrary to some findings . . . of previous efforts, portfolio assessment can have sufficient psychometric integrity to support purposes of public accounting'. (LeMahieu et al., 1995, p. 27, cited in Koretz , 1998, p. 323)

LeMahieu et al. attributed this to the fact that the moderation procedures were more rigorous than other systems. They had a team of expert assessors, mainly experienced classroom teachers, who double scored all the portfolios and arbitrated if they disagreed by more than one mark. They concluded,

> The lesson they draw for large-scale portfolio assessment seems to be that successful scoring requires efforts to engage all teachers in in-depth, extended, thoughtful discussions of the desired features of student work. Researchers on the Pittsburgh Arts PROPEL writing project cite their 'long-standing institutional effort to develop a common interpretative framework for examining and considering student writing', as the reasons their scores were more reliable. (LeMahieu et al., 1994, cited in Stecher, 1998, p. 346)

Yet Koretz threw doubt over even this assessment system over saying that ultimately it showed little more reliability than the Vermont portfolio when the results were aggregated in a particular way. As Wiliam (2009) comments, this brought about a turning point in portfolio assessment in the US. Yet whether or not the RAND Corporation, which had funded Koretz's research, had come up with such gloomy results it is likely that portfolio assessment was not 'objective' enough for an American audience (ibid., 2009).

What the research did not say, however, was that it was unpopular among those who used it. Although many teachers in both Kentucky and Vermont found the assessment too time consuming, the benefits outweighed the disadvantages. Stecher, arguing that,

> reformers believe that substituting portfolios for standardized multiple-choice tests will provide more meaningful information about student performance, which

will help teachers monitor students and communicate with parents. (Stecher, 1998, p. 335)

found that, for example,

> Ninety percent of Kentucky principals 'agreed' or 'strongly agreed' that 'writing portfolios have great instructional potential' (Pankratz, 1995, p. 5). Teachers who participated in California experiments with portfolios in language arts and mathematics indicated that the experience had a 'powerful impact on their understanding of what students can or should be learning and how they . . . might support that learning'. (Thomas et al., 1995, p. 57 cited Stecher, 1998, p. 339)

Stecher concludes,

> On balance, the benefits of portfolio assessment, including changes in curriculum and instruction, appear to outweigh the burdens, including additional demands on teacher and student time. This conclusion is supported by comments from principals and teachers in Vermont, who characterized the portfolio assessments as a 'worthwhile burden'. (Koretz et al., 1994 cited Stecher, 1998, p. 347)

Unfortunately large scale portfolio assessment has, for now at least, ended – though experiments have been tried in a number of other states including, Alaska, Arizona, California, Connecticut, Maryland, New Mexico, Oregon, Texas and Rhode Island among others. Yet,

> The standards of reliability that had been set by the SAT simply could not be matched with portfolios. While advocates might claim that the latter were more valid measurements of learning, the fact that the same portfolio would get different scores according to who did the scoring made their use for summative purposes impossible in the US context. (Wiliam, 2009, p. 178)

New Zealand

One clear articulation of the principle articulated by Mellon, that there is no point in judging whether or not someone can write well in timed conditions, was seen in New Zealand with the English Study Design, Certificate of Studies: English examination taken at the end of schooling. Sadly this too ended in 2004 but it is worth noting what it achieved. The English Study Design (ESD) was set up in Waikato University in 1997 as part of a project to see if

English could be assessed using course-based work as opposed to terminal examination.

What is interesting about one of the main accounts of the project, a book called *Resisting Qualification Reforms in New Zealand: The English Study Design as constructive dissent*, is that it is told by an English expert, Terry Locke. Locke not only taught English in New Zealand High schools, for a while he also taught English at university level, before ending up in the education department at the University in Waikato. Although he includes research from people who were asked to evaluate the procedures, particularly the moderation of the coursework, his version of events reads very differently from those writing about the US models of portfolio assessment, which tend to concentrate on statistical models. Locke's description relies much more on analysis of the content of the project than numerical evidence. He begins by explaining why he thought there was a need for course-based assessment in the first place.

As the title of Locke's book suggests, with the word 'Resisting' being the first word of the title, followed by 'dissent', part of the reason that the ESD set up a qualification was in reaction to the New Zealand Qualifications Authority (NZQA) National Qualification Framework (NQF). This was introduced in 1990. It oversaw the curriculum for all post-compulsory education, Years 12 and 13. It specified all requirements for schooling on a matrix on which it stated Unit Standards. A pupil did not gain a global figure for say English but a conglomeration of these Unit Standards. Then in 1999, the New Zealand government introduced a new secondary schools qualification – the National Certificate in Educational Achievement. Terry Locke, director of the ESD, saw these changes to the New Zealand curriculum, as part of a general trend towards the managerialism of education as seen in the UK and Australia (Locke, 2007) a kind of post-Fordism where everything could be ticked and measured and where everything was accountable. Those at the ESD felt that many of these Unit Standards, in fact the Unit Standards altogether, were in many ways inappropriate for the assessment of English.

> The New Zealand English teachers involved in the English Study Design Project, like their counterparts in England and Australia, had been asked to implement a new curriculum document which was partitioned into strands and tied, outcome by outcome, into a 'progression' of levels viewed by many educators as flawed. (ibid., p. xvii)

Despite these serious misgivings about the Unit Standards voiced by both the teacher union and people such as Irwin (20001999), Hall (2000) and Locke

(2001a and b) schools were obliged to undergo training for the new NCEA level 1 (Year 11) in 2002. But the ESD was to be 'constructive' in its 'dissent' So, being very concerned about the progress being made by the NCEA, they lobbied the university at Waikato to allow the participants in the project to set up their own qualification – the University of Waikato Certificate of Studies. The university agreed to ratify levels 2 and 3, and even more surprisingly the National Register of Quality Assured Qualifications said that they would include this qualification under the NCEA.

What the ESD teachers embarked upon is what Locke calls 'activist professionalism' (Locke, 2007, p. 22), a desire to stand up and be counted.

> It was clear that the willingness of English teachers and departments to go out on a limb and adopt the English Study Design at Year 12 was the result of feeling that their voices had been marginalised during the seven years of curriculum and assessment reform. (ibid., p. 23)

They were reasserting their right to be thought of as central to any reform process – that teachers, teacher educators and those involved in university education – should be at the core of changes in assessment and to 'the construction of what constitutes worthwhile knowledge (in English)' (ibid., p. 24) and not part of the new managerialist agenda. In so doing they were 'drawing attention to the context-bound constructedness of the reforms [and] the ESD project both drew attention to the process of discursive colonization and fostered the means of resisting it' (ibid., p. 24).

So how did they view English in the ESD? Terry Locke describes it as 'Critical Eclecticism' (ibid., p. 44). He takes this position because the people involved did not start from a theoretical position and put this into practice, rather they all came at the project with their own particular classroom practices and derived a theory for these positions. It should be said that they were quite influenced by the original, 1989 Victorian Certificate of Education (VCE) syllabus for English, particularly what work was required of a Year 12 or 13 pupil. Thus much of the structure of the CS was taken from this syllabus. It included: A work file, a writing folio, a response to a text, a language investigation project, a text investigation seminar and a communication project. Each of these had clear learning outcomes. For example under 'response to text' the learning outcomes included:

- read and enjoy a range of texts
- develop skills in constructing meanings

- think critically, through attentive reading, viewing and listening, about the ways in which texts position readers to adopt certain viewpoints and diregard others
- develop, by analysing the language features of a range of texts, a critical understanding of how these features impact upon a reader's response (ibid., p. 46)

Students were expected, in Year 12, to study four texts, three of which had to be print based, including a novel. In Year 13 the list included one play by Shakespeare. Their position remained eclectic because while the subject matter might seem to favour a cultural heritage approach, point four of the learning outcomes takes a rather more critically literate stance; reading and enjoying texts might have a strong element of personal growth. What is interesting to note, however, is that they just avoided using those terms, which seemed controversial. Under the new Unit driven NCEA, for example, writing was subdivided into three categories – expressive, transactional and poetic. Under the CS programme writing simply became writing.

What is significant is the way the coursework was moderated. There were several stages. It was moderated, in the first place, by the teachers, who taught the Year 12 classes. Next, every school had to appoint a school moderator. This person had to check that all the marking procedures were in place and that the Year 12 teachers had assessed the coursework accurately. Finally there was a panel of inter-school experts who sampled a batch of representative coursework from each centre. If these moderators decided that a school was to harsh or lenient in their grading then the school involved had to explain their decision-making and alter the grades accordingly.

But they included another element. They had a two-hour externally set exam on both reading and writing, which they included as a moderation device for the grading system as a whole. The idea came from the English advisor to the Auckland Region, Barry Gough and was based on a similar system for the Form 5 School Certificate. Because this had proved fairly popular in the past, the idea of a new test was readily accepted by the teachers in the ESD. Essentially this was to provide a kind of norm reference against which the entries of the schools involved could be measured.

Although the new test was accepted by teachers, the introduction of an exam in itself, was quite a controversial move not least because the exam was norm referenced. The way they marked the individual folders of work was not norm referenced. Locke does not describe the actual method that they used but we can assume that it was criterion referenced at the very least and probably construct referenced. Against this method the ESD were setting a norm-referenced test against which the schools were to be judged. Norm referencing had become outdated because it was assumed that it put a ceiling on what kind of grades could be given. For instance – if the curve fell a certain way then only so many could be given an 'A', a 'B' and so on. It was felt that students would not be given the grade they deserved only the grades that the norm-referenced curve allowed. This was part of the reason that the Unit Standards had been introduced, as a direct opposition to norm referencing. They were there to provide standards-based criteria. Locke defends the idea, however, saying that norm referencing provides a kind of precautionary guide as to how the grades will be distributed. In 1998, therefore, they set an exam called the reference test trial.

There were difficulties in setting the exam, not least in finding one reading passage that was suitable for multi-ethnic, urban and rural populations. The nature of the test then was always problematic and had it continued it was something that they would always check, on an annual basis. The exam was taken near the end of Year 12 and, as has already been said, comprised of two main components – a piece of writing, though they could choose the genre, and an unseen text for reading. It was marked with two criteria – 'content and context' and 'conventions of language'. The research project asked whether the test was an 'appropriate moderation device' and whether it was a 'suitable moderation device for close reading and writing' (ibid., p. 114). The research was carried out by an external evaluator on the project, Cedric Hall.

While Locke does not provide numbers in his analysis of the data, he records some interesting points. The fact that the course grades were higher than the test scores, in six out of the eight participating schools, did not necessarily mean that the course grades were wrong. This is possibly because the students felt that the test did not count in their final grade and therefore did not put as much effort into the test. It may also have been that the students had time to draft and redraft their pieces in the coursework, something not mentioned in the final report. Hall also found that while the external exams gave a satis-factory level of consistency, 'the estimates of the reliability of the moderation test were lower than that for teachers assessments' (Locke, 2007, p. 112).

This observation was also found in Hall's analysis of the 2003 Certificate of Studies (Hall, 2003). What was debated by the English Programme Committee was whether or not this should affect the pupils grades overall – the norm referencing question. Locke writes,

> In its deliberations, the EPC adopted various 'norms' as diagnostic guides in examining whether its results were more or less on target. For Year 12, for example, it set 'guiding percentages' of 15 per cent for students gaining a 'merit'

pass and 5 per cent for gaining excellence. However, the EPC saw these 'norms' as guiding figures only – changes would not be made to grade distributions unless there was a case for doing so. (ibid., p. 117)

In the end no changes were made in 2003. What the tests did show, however, was whether schools were lenient or severe relative to the examination. This proved particularly pertinent in the last year that the exam was taken, in 2004. Hall had suggested, for example, that a school which varied considerably from the test ought to have the grades changed, if the test had proved too hard for that school, for example, but was not too difficult in and of itself. As a result, in 2004, 'Two schools had their percentages deducted and one had a percentage added for Year 12 Response to Text. One school had a percentage deducted for Year 12 Writing' (ibid., p. 117). This, for Locke, was an indication that the reference tests worked as a moderation device.

The Certificate of Study, however, did not survive beyond 2004. There were a number of reasons for this. One was that the government, in effect, demanded double payment for entry; the other – that they would not include the results in the overall scores for university entrance. This was because rather than giving numerous unit standards for their English, the ESD gave one overall grade. Although schools were incredibly sympathetic to the overall aims of the ESD, they could not jeopardise the future of their pupils. The dominance, therefore, of the unit standards and the government's NZQA had won.

Australia

Australia, rather like the States, up until recently, has had a strong federal system. In all there are eight states, although some are rather confusingly called territories. They are: Queensland, New South Wales, Victoria, Tasmania, south Australia and western Australia – and the two territories – the Australian Capital Territory and the Northern Territory. They have been keen to be independent, despite the low overall population of Australia because of the vast distances involved in administration. There can be over a thousand miles between say Sydney and some outlying settlement. It is after all a continent. Qualifications in Victoria, therefore, differ from those in New South Wales or Queensland. Pupils from one state can go to a university in another, though usually they do not, but the exams they take are very different.

The need for a national curriculum, however, has long been debated. The Conservative prime minister, John Howard, had attempted it in the 1990s but although he made some headway at a federal level he was blocked when it came to the individual states and so it looked as though it had been avoided. Yet in 2008 the National Assessment Programme – Literacy and Numeracy (NAPLAN) was introduced. Pupils in Years 3, 5, 7 and 9 had to take a national test in reading, writing and language conventions including spelling, grammar and punctuation as well as numeracy. This, rather like the Sats in England, was introduced so that the government, among others, could monitor national standards across time and was the first countrywide assessment programme. Perhaps more importantly, or certainly as important, on arriving in office Kevin Rudd, the new Labour prime minister, having declared that he was going to bring about an 'education revolution', introduced the idea, again, of a national curriculum. The board, overseeing the project, is chaired by a Professor Barry McGraw. The curriculum should finally come online in 2011 and is, at the moment, going through the traditional consultation phase.

So far there is a document for English, which is called the *Shape of the Australian Curriculum: English* (2009). Its first aim is that: 'The national English curriculum will be the basis of planning, teaching and assessment of English in Australian schools and will guide the work of both experienced and beginning teachers of English' (ibid,. p. 4). At the moment, however, there has been no impact on the way subjects are assessed in Years 11 and 12, the post compulsory phase of education. This is particularly pertinent in Queensland, where the Year 12 exam is entirely teacher moderated. As they put it themselves,

> Queensland follows a system of externally-moderated school-based assessment. Senior students are taught and assessed by their teachers in accordance with the requirements of Years 11 and 12 syllabuses. The QSA ensures that the curriculum and assessment programs developed by schools are rigorous and meet the requirements of the syllabuses. Teachers' judgments about the standards achieved by their students are moderated by the QSA using trained expert panels of teachers from other schools. (Queensland, 2009a)

Queensland has had a system of 100 per cent teachers' assessment since the 1970s. It came into being initially because there was little confidence in the reliability and validity of externally set exams. Various reports went into setting it up, including the Radford Report (1970), which resulted in an act of the state parliament introducing 100 per cent coursework in 1971. The argument was that it produced more 'penetrating' results than external exams. The Scott Report (1978), which was asked to review the progress of coursework, produced Review of School-based Assessment in Queensland Secondary Schools (ROSBA). They suggested that a review panel of expert teachers, rather than just school-based teachers, was a better arrangement for moderating pupils' work and that students' achievements should be criterion based rather than norm referenced. By 1985 this was in place.

All this shows a high degree of support from the state authority, unlike the New Zealand model or the ones in the US. The Queensland government constantly asked and still asks for reviews into the reliability of the system. Royce Sadler reviewed the system twice – in 1986 and again in 1993. Masters and McBryde (1994) found a correlation of 0.94 per cent agreement between markers, greater than that found among markers in external exams. The model for assessment in Queensland, then, aims for a criterion led assessment with 'respect for teacher professionalism in judging student achievement' (Cummings and Maxwell, 2004, p. 93).

What is interesting about the review panel model is that it is very similar to that operated by the JMB/NEAB now the AQA. Both have first, schools and then, expert teachers moderating the pupils' work.

> The system of moderation is based on a close partnership between the QSA and the schools. The QSA contributes the design, operation and servicing of the structures that allow the system to operate. It accepts the responsibility for training the people who serve on review panels to review school work programs and student results. On their part, schools contribute the services of teachers as review panellists, and are responsible for developing and implementing work programs in line with syllabuses, and for assessing students' work against statewide standards. They collect the student work samples and data necessary for their students to receive Senior Certificates. (Queensland, cited in ibid., 2004, p. 95)

With this system, they believe that,

> Authority subjects taught in schools are of the highest possible standards, student results in the same subject are comparable across the state, and match the requirements of the syllabus, and the process used is transparent and publicly accountable. (ibid., p. 95)

Not content with the moderation system they also have randomized sampling of assessments, completed annually, and have done so since 1994. This provides a further check on the school-based moderation although it is completed after the pupils have left school and does not alter their grades. As the *Random Sampling of Assessment in Authority Subjects* (2009) puts it:

> The principal purpose is to evaluate the quality of school-based assessment programs and the comparability of teacher judgments of student achievement in Authority subjects across the state after Senior Education Profiles (SEPs), including Queensland Certificates of Education (QCEs) and Senior Statements, have been issued. The key question for the random sampling project is therefore:
>   How consistently do teachers apply statewide standards in determining students' levels of achievement in Authority subjects? (Queensland, 2009b p. 5)

In English, as in previous years, the random sampling was good.

What is most impressive about it is the way, according to proponents of the system, that it blurs the distinctions between formative and summative assessment. Graham Maxwell, a one-time deputy director in Queensland's Study Authority, claims that the assessment system becomes progressive, one assignment builds on the one before it.

> The point about progressive assessment is not that there are several assessments distributed over a period of time but that later assessments allow further improvement on knowledge and skills that were also assessed in earlier assessments . . . This operates like a spiral curriculum . . .
>   As the student builds up the portfolio of evidence of their performance, earlier assessments may be superseded by later assessments covering the same underlying dimensions of learning. (Maxwell, 2004, p. 3)

While this was undoubtedly the case in other portfolio type assessments, Maxwell actually points this out. It was certainly the case with a 100 per cent coursework under the NEAB. Pupils had, for example, to do a piece on a twentieth-century playwright and, typically over the course of two years, they did two. The second piece of work that they produced on the playwright that they studied was almost invariably better than the first.

Wynne Harlen, in discussing the Queensland system both in the EPPI review (2005) and in her 2004 article claims that the Queensland system is different in that the classroom teachers do not have the ultimate say in a pupil's grade and that it is decided by the review panel. This means, effectively, the class teacher does not have control of a pupil's summative assessment, meaning that the formative process of the classroom is separated from the summative purposes of an examiner, in this case a review panel member. Maxwell's claim that formative and summative assessment merge, therefore, is not strictly true. It is, however, the class teacher who makes the first grading on a pupil's work, and, provided nobody disagrees with it, this stands, thus making it the kind of progressive assessment or spiral curriculum that Maxwell describes.

Queensland, then has the ultimate high stakes assessment, in that the results for these tests provide entrance into tertiary education, and yet they are entirely school based. They are concerned about the reliability of this system and have put in place ways of ensuring this. The benefits to the validity of course-based assessments can be summed up in Pitman, O'Brien and Mc Callow (1999) study, which shows that ultimately it benefits assessment for learning and Sadler's (2006) study on guild knowledge. For now, at least, The Queensland system is staying put.

Conclusion

An albeit rough glance at these three modes of course-based assessment shows that the biggest hurdle to overcome is the culture of assessment, especially a political one. It seems that state or national governments put more weight on assessments being reliable than valid. In the case of the United States it was both the rhetoric that surrounded assessment in general and at state level in particular that meant that the portfolio system ended. There were too many fears about the reliability of moderation that meant that testing was brought back in a more traditional form. It might be said that insufficient care was given when the Vermont State testing was organized. Having looked at the model given by the NEAB they did not adopt it, which meant that the reliability of their moderation was not what it might have been. This was particularly foolish given the culture of test reliability in the US.

In New Zealand, although the ETS had shown that the assessment arrangements that they had could be made reliable, the New Zealand government, in effect, decided that testing pupils through individual Unit Standards was preferable. To have a maverick exam, which assessed pupils' ability in English as a whole, in the middle of the neat talk of Unit Standards, was messy. Only Queensland still maintains a portfolio method of assessment.

Looking Forward

8

Chapter Outline

English continues to remain controversial because there is always a conflict about what it is for and more recently, whether or not pupils are being aided in what they produce by either the internet or anxious parents. Three new forms of summative assessment are about to come in that illustrate this point – functional skills, national sample tests and the new GCSE. In a few years time it may be something different again but they are indicative of any government's desire to ensure that tests are seen to be reliable and that they quell the business and the general public's perpetual need to see that standards remain high.

Functional skills

Sir Terry Leahy, chief executive of Britain's largest private employer, said on the day before the KS3 Sats were abandoned that, 'No one can deny that Britain has spawned a generation of young people who struggle to read, write or do simple maths'(Leahy, 2009). In so doing he was hardly being original. He echoes countless businessmen over numerous generations.

The Newbolt report in 1921, for example, quoting Boots Pure Drug Co. commented that, 'The teaching of English in present day schools produces a very limited command of the English language' (Newbolt Report, Ch. 3, para 77, p. 72). In the same report all but a few employers complained that they had found difficulty in 'obtaining employees who can speak and write English clearly and correctly' (ibid., ch. 3, para 77, p. 72).

Seven years later little had changed. The Spens Report of 1928 wrote, 'It is a common and grave criticism that many pupils pass through grammar school without acquiring the capacity to express themselves in English' (cited in Cox, 1995, p. 38). The Norwood Report of 1943 claimed to have received 'strong evidence of the poor quality of English of Secondary School pupils . . . the evidence is such as to leave no doubt in our minds that we are confronted by a serious failure of secondary schools' (ibid., p. 38). As Colin MacCabe pointed out, 'It is notorious that educational standards, and particularly literacy, seem to fall with such monotonous regularity from generation to generation that it is a wonder that anybody reads at all' (MacCabe, 1990, p. 7).

The government's answer, of whatever complexion, to such complaints, is always to talk of basics and this in part explains the Functional Skills Standards. Functional Skills, officially came in as a result of The Tomlinson Report on 14- to 19-year-olds (2004). Tomlinson advocated the abolition of A-levels and vocational qualifications to see them replaced by a diploma. He wanted to integrate the academic with the vocational so that the age-old divide between them would disappear. You would not know if someone had taken a vocational or academic route in, for example, the media. In fact your final qualification might combine elements from both branches and no one would be able to tell.

Under Tomlinson's model, the test burden in secondary education was to be considerably reduced from its current load. GCSE's were to be part of the diploma structure and there was to be more trust placed in teacher assessment. He advocated a

> move to a system of assessment based on the professional judgement of teachers and tutors [which] would reduce significantly the overall burden associated with external examinations, allowing resources to be redeployed within the system and creating more time for teaching and learning. (Tomlinson, 2004, p. 86)

Unfortunately he also recommended literacy and numeracy tests, which could be taken at any point when the pupil was ready. Almost as soon as it was published, however, Tomlinson was rejected. The Government decided to retain both A-levels and, as significantly, the functional skills tests. These have now been through many forms. For example in their draft form they were defined thus:

> The initial stage in the process of defining a qualification . . . for the purposes of ensuring that the content of knowledge, understanding and skills developed is captured. They allow the scope, content, level of demand and parameters of the areas of knowledge, understanding and skills to be defined. (QCA, 2006b, p. 2)

There is nothing intrinsically objectionable in any of the draft standards themselves, nothing one could quarrel with – except the tone. This is, as the title suggests, functional. At the highest level, for example, the learning outcome of reading is defined as, 'Read, understand and compare texts and use them to gather information, ideas, arguments and opinions'.(ibid., p. 8) Writing is similarly drab – pupils must be able to 'Write documents communicating information, ideas and opinions effectively'(ibid., p. 10) – while the learning outcome of good speaking and listening is, 'Make a range of contributions to discussion and make effective presentations' (ibid., p. 6).

This then is a joyless document, not wrong just atomistic and somewhat arid. In one of the latest documents, which talks about the pilot schemes which run until summer 2010, the QCA writes that, 'People with good functional skills are able to complete everyday tasks competently, whether it's writing a clear, formal letter, finding information online or working out the cost of an order' (QCA, 2009b, p. 2). Again the emphasis, while optimistic, is practical not imaginative or creative.

In defining functional skills they write,

> Functional skills are the essential elements of English, mathematics and ICT that equip individuals to operate confidently, effectively and independently in life and at work. The full functional skills qualifications in English, mathematics and ICT will be introduced in September 2010 and will become a vital part of the personal development of all learners. Functional skills will be highly valued by both employers and higher education providers for their impact on productivity, independence and achievement. (ibid., p. 3)

It is the fact that they say that they are the 'essential elements of English' that might make one flinch just slightly. Once more it skews the English curriculum away from the notion that the subject is about the art of language and towards a syllabus that prioritizes somewhat arid technical skills. This should not, of course, be a debate that revolves around questions of either/or. Accuracy is important in effective communication. But creativity, pleasure and the imagination are central to the English curriculum and these are mentioned not once.

The QCA go on to write, 'The new secondary curriculum emphasizes those problem-solving approaches, which means that functional skills learning in schools may take place in "traditional" English, mathematics and ICT lessons' (ibid., p. 3). They even try and make it appealing to teachers by claiming that 'Many existing teaching practices are well suited to this approach, including learner-centred and problem-centred approaches, active learning, partnership learning and assessment for learning' (ibid., p. 3).

Two pages later, however, in 'Top ten steps to success', under point seven, they say:

> Make the most of the opportunity to introduce innovative approaches to teaching – learners are responding enthusiastically to the fact that functional skills are different from 'traditional' English, mathematics and ICT learning. (ibid., p. 5)

And also, 'Give learners opportunities to practise assessment – don't assume that a high-achieving GCSE learner will find functional skills easy, for example' (ibid., p. 5). Throughout the document it does not define the 'traditional' but, one suspects, it would involve more of the imaginative and less of the life skills that are promoted by the functional skills programme. As one of the institutions on the pilot scheme says, 'The beauty of the Diploma and functional skills is that young people are learning things that will be of real value to them in the future' (ibid., p. 16). Like Gradgrind in the Victorian era they do not, apparently deal in 'Fairy Palaces' (Dickens, 1854, 1980, p. 28).

Initially everyone who did a GCSE was going to have to have a Functional Skills grade 2 if they were to achieve a grade 'C' at GSCE. This, however, was going to be difficult. Even in the pilot scheme schools had found it problematic. In Simon Langton Grammar School for Boys, for instance, the assistant head found that, 'The transition to functional skills has proved trickier for mathematics and English' (QCA, 2009b, p. 14). Although they entered all the boys for the functional skills test they found that only 85 per cent achieved a level 2. They realized that their,

> Learners needed more time to practise and prepare for the specific nature of functional skills assessment. The oral component has proved challenging

logistically in English because functional skills presentations are different from GCSE presentations. (ibid., p. 14)

Again it is the fact that they had 'to practise and prepare for the specific nature of the functional skills assessment' that is worrying. Far from being integrated into 'traditional' English lessons, therefore, the demands are very 'different' (ibid., p. 5) even in speaking and listening.

The requirement that functional skills needed to take place along side GCSE was abandoned and for many this was a relief. Recently, however, it has been said that the new Report Card, that was recommended by the Expert Group on Assessment, will require all schools to take the functional skills tests as part of the publications that the school has to make. This means that once more schools will have to grapple with how to integrate the functional with the creative. More worrying still, it will also mean that pupils on the diploma track will possibly only taking these exams. This will mean that there is a danger that those pupils who most need convincing of the pleasure of narrative, or the release enjoyed in writing something that matters to them, may never have the opportunity. They will be consigned to classes in which they are drilled in the mechanics of English to get them through a test. Their imagination will remain unstimulated; their creativity stifled. And all this because, the likes of Terry Leahy, think that 'Britain has spawned a generation of young people who struggle to read, write or do simple maths'.

National sample tests at fourteen

We await, with somewhat nervous apprehension, the national tests, which are due to come in 2012. Again an idea proposed by the Expert Group on Assessment KS3 Sats, are to be replaced, in theory by a sampling of around 10,000 pupils aged 14 to assess whether or not standards in English have risen or fallen over time (DCSF, 2009, p. 11). This in itself is somewhat problematic as the results will not be known to the individuals or even the schools that are taking them. Motivation to do well in them might, therefore, be a trifle curtailed.

Nevertheless, the tests are intended to assess the whole of theKS3 curriculum. Simon Gibbons, writing on them attempted to be optimistic

In its best form, a national sampling test would aim to assess the full curriculum. Clearly this can't be done in one sitting, but in different years, perhaps, different areas of the curriculum might be the focus for the assessment, so that over time information might emerge about coverage of and standards in the various elements of English. Alternatively, in a given year, tests focused on different areas of the subject might be taken by different students or different schools to allow a broad picture to emerge of standards across the breadth of the curriculum. The breadth to be assessed would – within the three main attainment targets of Speaking and Listening, Reading and Writing – include fiction and non fiction; modern and classic literature; Shakespeare; poetry, prose and drama texts; media and moving image; drama and ICT. (Gibbons, submitted)

He argues for a system of 'accredited assessors' who, 'Might be able to carry out forms of assessment that genuinely did start to get at achievement across the breadth of the English curriculum'(ibid.). But the idea of pencil and paper tests loom. Out will have gone Sats in one guise and in they will come through another, albeit with a sample of children. Although the QCDA might say they are interested in sampling the whole curriculum, therefore, it might be that they are only keen to see whether or not pupils have got the 'basics' of literacy right.

GCSE

Finally, two new GCSEs come into being in 2010 – English Language and English Literature. Although the new GCSE will not be cluttered with the functional skills test it still pays a kind of lip service to those who are anxious about standards of English given that they have a whole GCSE that is once more dedicated to the study of 'language'. But to consider the full implications of the new exams we must cast our minds back to the beginnings of the national curriculum.

In 1989 one of the things that was significant about the GCSE was that it combined English Language with English Literature. The new GCSE was called just English. In the past literature, which had only been awarded at O-level, was taken by the elite of the elite. Not everyone who took O-level was entered for the literature exam, some just took language. At CSE it was combined. Students did have to look at at least one book but they did not have to look, for example, at any Shakespeare, or even poetry. Nor did those pupils who just sat the English language O-level.

All that changed with the national curriculum. Everyone now had to study literature and what was more the vast majority of schools decided that they might as well enter all students for the literature GCSE as well. This was because there could be overlap between the two exams. Shakespeare, for example, appeared in both the English GCSE and the literature paper. So did the novel. All this could be combined when submitting candidates' work which, initially could be done through 100 per cent coursework. Even when 100 per cent coursework was abolished the basic curriculum remained the same. Some aspects became more precise, such as having to do a comparison between a twentieth- and pre-twentieth century text for literature, but in essence pupils were still studying literature and language combined.

This was important because it said that English was about more than the technical, about the correct use of grammar, it was about how language was used to say something both in their own writing and in analysing authors' works. Although only 20 per cent of the GCSE English, and 30 per cent of the literature, was now coursework, far more time went into producing it than was actually called for. This was because much formative practice went into the writing, which in the end had a beneficial effect on the pupils' performance in general. If we think of the piece of coursework done on *Romeo and Juliet* in Chapter 4, for example, as a result of peer assessment, the pupil will write better on *Romeo and Juliet* but they will also have an idea of how to organize and write better about any piece of literature that is put in front of them. Over the course of two years, then, pupils improved in their performance considerably.

There is a fear that this will change with the new GCSEs and this is a subject to which we shall return. For one of the biggest worries is whether or not most pupils will take the literature exam. There will be a general English exam which will combine literature and language and then also two other exams – a language and a literature exam. If the straight English exam is taken then the literature exam cannot be taken with it. This is a concern as many pupils may take just this GCSE and no others. It is like the science options where one either takes three GCSEs or a joint double science. The difference is that English is only counted as one subject not two when combined.

The GCSE in literature must be taken with the language exam and cannot be taken alone. The GCSE language exam, however, can also replace the English but, in order to get five grades 'A*' – 'C', including maths and English, it is the language exam not the literature one that counts. A 'B', therefore, in literature and a 'D' for language will be meaningless. It is a concern, then, that pupils who are on the borderline between 'C' and 'D' will only be entered for language or the straight English exam. This problem is amplified by the fact that there is intended to be less overlap between the English and language and literature exams.

And this has been reinforced by the changes boards have had to put in place to be accredited. Initially, for example, the AQA had a cluster of overlapping texts for English, language and literature in their controlled assignments thus making it quite flexible until the last minute which exam you would be entered for. (I will explain controlled assignments shortly). The QCDA has altered this so there is virtually no overlap (Gibbons, 2010). Pupils will have to study different texts for each exam again making it more likely that only an elite will study literature and language and the majority will do English alone. It will almost be impossible not to decide the course at the beginning of the GCSE rather than late on. In many ways this is a turning the clock back 30 years to the old O-level and CSE where the privileged studied books and the rest did CSE.

It is the controlled assignments, however, that are possibly causing the most anxiety. In the past pupils have been able to complete their coursework at home. This has caused huge anxiety in the press for two reasons. The first is that middle-class parents help their offspring with their coursework, and it is feared, do a great deal of it themselves. The other is the internet – pupils copy work from it. So great was the anxiety that in 2006 the QCA published a document called *Authenticating Coursework* (QCA, 2006a). As we have seen, in Chapter 6, however, English teachers do not appear to be as worried as the politicians, press or public that pupils cheat. Satisfied that they see enough of their work to decide whether or not an essay has come off the internet or a parent has had too great a hand in the writing of it, they are not concerned about it.

But the government, and, therefore, the QCDA are worried. When they came to rewrite the syllabi for GCSE they introduced something called a controlled assignment. At first glance it would appear that it is a return to a greater proportion of coursework. Certainly in the English exam 40 per cent is now done in controlled conditions and 20 per cent is for Speaking and Listening. This means that 60 per cent of the GCSE is done in class and only 40 per cent in formal terminal exams. There is, however, a catch. Controlled conditions does not mean that a piece of coursework is now carried out in class, it means that the coursework is like another exam only this time it is done in lesson time.

So anxious are they that no cheating can take place that the QCDA have stipulated that pupils can only take in very brief notes on what they have done in class to the, what is in effect, test. If we look, for example, at the AQA syllabus we find, for example, that pupils have to complete three tasks amounting to 1600 words on 'Understanding Creative Texts'. In this they have to write about a Shakespeare text, the English literary heritage and work from other cultures. If we remember the piece of work from Chapter 4, which was a peer assessed piece on Shakespeare, it would be hard to see how that could be done under the new regime. Certainly peer assessment would be possible but not at all in the same way. Even if the pupil could take in the comments that their peer made on their work, they would have to memorize the text that they had written because they would not be allowed to take that in to the exam.

At its worst this will lead to very poor habits. The temptation to drill students as to what they have to do will be very great. Because, in effect, teachers know the answers to a controlled conditioned assignment they could so arrange it that for a poetry assignment, for instance, all the relevant quotes are underlined and all the key literary terms spelled out. They could organize the paragraphs in numerical order so that the essay would seem to have a logical progression. They could even have topic sentences for each one. In other words, short of writing the essay for them teachers would control the writing of them very closely indeed. In fact if a pupil had a good memory they could learn an essay off by heart, from the internet, and reproduce it in class and it would be much harder to accuse them of cheating because they would have done it without apparently consulting a computer. Far from avoiding cheating through coursework, therefore, this exam would seem to aid it.

In addition, the other problem with controlled assignments is when exactly they will be done. If we take again the English exam for AQA, pupils have to complete a minimum of five controlled assignments. Presumably these will each have to be done at the end of the unit of work, but it will also mean that it will be much harder for pupils to redo an assignment as it has to be done in classroom conditions.

NATE and Durham University

The functional skills test and the new GCSE are just two examples of what can happen when a government intervenes in the assessment process. In trying to allay fears, for example, of cheating they have, possibly, made it easier to do. Even if they have not they will make English a more tedious subject as will the attempt to examine pupils' functional skills.

But English teachers still persist in trying to get a more holistic assessment of their subject. The most recent attempt was made by NATE and the Curriculum, Evaluation and Management (CEM) Centre at Durham University. Called the NATE/ Durham pilot assessment project this was work which, like KOSAP, concentrated on KS3 (Gibbons and Marshall, 2010). NATE was approached by the centre, in December 2008, to organize a trial of coursework assessment. NATE met in January 2009, with Peter Tymms, from Durham, to determine how they would go about it. In many respects the project had more in common with the early LATE attempts to assess pupil work than the JMB or even KOSAP.

To begin with it was agreed that all pupils should answer from a set stimulus. In this case it was a picture, by Degas, from the National Gallery. Simon Gibbons, the NATE representative, suggested several ways in to the painting but teachers could, if they wanted chose their own, as long as it was based on the picture. Next came the marking. Gibbons originally had a mark scheme out of 24, much like the GCSE mark scheme. He then subdivided it into seven categories from 0–3, 'Where there is a response, little or no sense of meaning is conveyed' to 22–4 where, 'The writing is confident'. In its way this was an attempt to keep the assessment holistic, although technical accuracy was important. For example, in marks 7–9 Gibbons put, 'Monosyllabic words generally spelt correctly. Misspellings are phonetically plausible'. More common were criterion like 'Writing is lively and thoughtful' or 'Writing is interesting and engages the reader'.

This system of assessing was changed, however, at the behest of CEM before the teachers involved actually saw them. In the January 2009 meeting a new rubric for marking was proposed which had four criteria and were arranged somewhat like the APP, where each criterion was assessed against a level. National curriculum levels were not, however, used. The criteria were: general writing quality; creativity, vocabulary and divergence; punctuation and paragraphing; spelling.

These four criteria were discussed at the January meeting and modified to three: general writing quality/impact on reader; writer's choices; cohesion and coherence.

What is interesting about these is that they omit any strict adherence to technical accuracy – in particular punctuation, paragraphing and spelling. They are implied in the criterion cohesion and coherence but not explicitly stated. It is implied to in general writing quality, even, to an extent, in writer's choices. In this way technical accuracy is seen to have its place in a variety of ways, spread over, but not specifically within, one criterion (see Sadler, 1989). To this extent a more holistic approach is again being taken, though the fact that they were specific criteria makes it not unlike James Britton's first attempt at assessing before he considered rapid impression marking. Marks had to be given for each criterion and while a global comment could be made there was no overall grade given. Curiously, it was also agreed that there should be no age limit on the pupils. In other words this was not being done by Year 8 pupils, for example, but could be done with any Year, 7, 8 or 9, within KS3.

Although 23 people were interested in doing the project at first, in the end only 9 people actually took part. Two sets of marks were taken. The teacher marked their own class's work and then submitted the essays and marks to Durham. CEM then redistributed the essays to other people who were taking part. The second marker, then marked essays from three or four different teachers. All essays and marks were then collated by the Durham team and the results were presented to the teachers involved in November 2009.

The results were somewhat similar to the early LATE trials in that although the marking was similar there were a few outliers on individual criterion. What was not given was a sense of how people thought the pupils had done overall. Whether or not this would have made a difference is not altogether clear. Again what the Durham team seemed interested was reliability more than the validity of the tests. In terms of reliability, however, there did appear to be some among the more experienced markers. This in itself confirms that marking is something that gets better with time (see Protherough et al., 1989).

Conclusion

What then do we learn from the turbulence that marks out English and assessment. The main thing is hope. Despite over a 150 years of battle English teachers are still trying to assess English in a way that makes sense to them. Confronted with 'A [department] of facts and calculations . . . With a rule and a pair of scales, and the multiplication table always in [their] pocket, sir, ready to weigh and measure any parcel of human nature' (Dickens, 1854, 1980, p. 10) they will always seek to develop the world of creativity and imagination.

From the battles with the London Board through the confrontation with the government over Sats English to the trials with KOSAP or Durham, English teachers will ask whether or not the government, of whatever hue, or the exam boards, or the QCDA have got it right. What keeps them going is the hope that one day someone will listen and say 'You may have got a point'.

Briefly, in the great scheme of things, on occasion they have. The trials that were started by the JMB in the 60s, which lasted for about 25 years, and ended with a 16+ exam, which assessed everybody, went someway to producing a holistic assessment in English for all. Continual complaints about the basics, the internet and cheating have got in the way. Now teachers have to grapple with controlled conditions exams and APP in a way that makes it hard to remember why they taught English in the first place.

Like so many of the teachers in this book my first real love is language – its rhythms and cadence, its capacity to create meaning for the author and audience alike. It is about English as an art. No matter how the functional is taught, or the basics covered the wonders of English cannot be fitted in to a tick box on correctness. But how such a love is to be taught is quite another matter – it requires rigour and thought. It needs Dewey's 'high organisation based upon ideas' (Dewey, 1966, pp. 28–9). But, 'To be truly artistic, a work must be aesthetic – that is framed for enjoyed receptive perception' (Dewey, 2005, p. 49).

References

Abbs, P. (1982) *English Within the Arts: A Radical Alternative for English and the Arts in the Curriculum*, London: Hodder and Stoughton.

Alexander, R. (2006a) *Towards Dialogic Teaching: Rethinking Classroom Talk*. Cambridge: Dialogos.

Alexander, R. (2006b) *Education as Dialogue: Moral and Pedagogical Choices for a Runaway World*. Cambridge: Dialogos.

Almond, D. (15 July 1999) *The Independent*.

Arnold, M. (1869, 1948) *Culture and Anarchy*, J. Dover Wilson (ed.), Cambridge: Cambridge University Press.

Arnold, M. (1867, 1979) *Selected Poetry and Prose*, D. Thompson (ed.), London: Heineman.

Assessment Reform Group (2002) *Assessment for Learning: 10 Principles*, Cambridge: University of Cambridge School of Education.

Association of Teachers and Lecturers (1996) *Level Best Revisited: An Evaluation of the Statutory Assessment in 1996*, London: ATL Publications.

Baker, M. (1994) *Who Rules Our Schools*, London: Hodder and Stoughton.

Ball, S. J., Kenny, A. and Gardiner, D. (1990) 'Literacy policy and the teaching of English'. In I. Goodson and P. Medway (eds) *Bringing English to Order*, London: Falmer, 47–66.

Balls, E. (2008). 'Major reforms to school accountability including an end to compulsory national tests for fourteen year olds. More support in year 7 to help children make the jump to secondary school'. London: Department for Children, Schools and Families. Retrieved 8 December 2008 from http://www.dcsf.gov.uk/pns/DisplayPN.cgi?pn_id=2008_0229.

Barnes, D., Britten, J. and Rosen, H. (1972) *Language, the Learner and the School*, Middlesex: Penguin Books.

Barrs, M and Cook, V. (2002) *The Reader in the Writer*. London: CLPE.

Black, P. and Wiliam, D. (1998a) 'Assessment and classroom learning'. *Assessment in Education: Principles Policy and Practice*, **5** (1), 7–73.

Black, P. and Wiliam, D. (1998b) *Inside the Black Box*. London: NFER Nelson.

Black, P. and Wiliam, D. (2006). 'The reliability of assessments'. In J. Gardner (ed.), *Assessment and learning* (pp. 119–31), London: Sage.

Black, P. and Wiliam, D. (2009) 'Developing the theory of formative assessment'. *Educational Assessment, Evaluation and Accountability*, **21** (1), 5–31.

Black, P. J., Harrison, C., Lee, C., Marshall, B. and Wiliam, D. (2003) *Assessment for Learning: Putting It into Practice*, Buckingham: Open University Press.

Bolon, C. (2000) 'School-based Standard Testing. Education Policy Archives'. **8** (23) In D. Wiliam, (2009) *Assessment for Learning: Why No Profile in US Policy*, London: Sage.

Britton, J. (1950) *Report on the Meaning and Marking of Imaginative Compositions*. London: LATE.

Britton, J. (1955) 'The paper in English Language at Ordinary Level'. *Use of English* **6** (3), 178–84. In S. Gibbons (2009) 'Back to the Future: A case study'. *English in Education* **43** (1), 19–31.

Britton, J. (1964) *The Multiple Marking of Compositions*, London: HMSO.

Britton, J. (1974) *Language and Learning*, Middlesex: Penguin Books.

Britton, J. and Martin, N. (1989) 'English Teaching – Is it a Profession?' *English and Education*, **23** (2), 1–8.

Carlyle, T. (1829, 1986) *Selected Writings*, New York: Penguin.

Chartered Institute of Educational Assessment (2009) http://www.ciea.org.uk.

Christie, F. and Misson, R. (1998) 'Framing the Issues in Literacy Education'. In F. Christie, and R. Misson (eds) *Literacy and Schooling*, London: Routledge.

Close, G., Furlong, T. and Swain, J. (1995) *The Validity KS2 of the 1996 Key Stage 2 Tests in English Maths and Science: A Report Commissioned by the Association of Teachers and Lecturers*, London: King's College London School of Education.

Coffey, J., Sato, M. and Thiebault, M. (2005) 'Classroom assessment up close – and personal'. *Teacher Development*, **9** (2), 169–84.

Coles, J. (2003) 'Alas poor Shakespeare: Teaching and testing at KS3'. *English in Education* **37** (3), 3–12.

Coles, J. (2004) 'Much ado about nationhood and culture: Shakespeare and the search for an 'English' identity'. *Changing English* **11** (1), March 47–58.

Coles, J. (2009) 'Testing Shakespeare to the limit: Teaching Macbeth in a year 9 classroom'. *English in Education*, **43** (1), 32–49.

Cooper, P. and Davies, C. (1993) 'The Impact of National Curriculum Assessment Arrangements on English Teachers' thinking and classroom practice in Secondary English schools'. *Teaching and Teacher Education*, **9** (5/6), 559–70.

Corden, R. (2000) *Literacy and Learning through Talk: Strategies for the Primary Classroom*. Buckingham: Open University Press.

Cox, B. (1995) *Cox on the Battle for the English Curriculum*, London: Hodder and Stoughton.

Creber, P. (1990) *Thinking through English*, Milton Keynes: Open University Press.

Cumming, J. J. and Maxwell, G. S. (2004) 'Profiles of educational assessment systems worldwide'. *Assessment in Education: Principles, Policy & Practice*, **11** (1), 89–108.

Daugherty. (2004a). *Jane Davidson Receives Daugherty Group's Final Report*. Retrieved 8 December 2008 from http://new.wales.gov.uk/news/archivepress/educationpress/edpress04/706492/?l ang=en.

Daugherty, R. (2004b) *Learning Pathways through Statutory Assessment: Key Stages 2 and 3. Final Report of Daugherty Assessment Review Group*, Cardiff: Welsh Assembly Government.

Daugherty, R. and Ecclestone, K. (2009) 'Constructing Assessment for Learning in the UK Policy Environment'. In J. Gardener (ed.), *Assessment and Learning*, London: Sage.

Davidson, K. (11 July 2008) Article. *Times Educational Supplement*.

Departmental Committttee of the Board of Education [The Newbolt Report] (1921) *The Teaching of English in England: Being the Report of the Departmental Committee Appointed by the President of the Board of Education to Inquire into the Position of English in the Educational System of England,* London: HMSO.

Department for Children, Schools and Families (2008). *The Assessment for Learning Strategy,* London: DCSF.

Department for Children, Schools and Families (2009). *The Report of the Expert Group on Assessment,* London: DCSF.

Department for Education and Skills (2003). *Key Stage 3 Strategy. Foundation Subjects Strand: Key Messages about Assessment for Learning,* London: DfES.

Department for Education and Skills (2004a) *Assessment for Learning: Subject Development Materials,* London: DfES.

Department for Education and Skills [The Tomlinson Report] (2004b) *Pedagogy and Practice: Teaching and Learning in Secondary Schools Unit 12: Assessment for Learning.* London: DfES, (2004) *14–19 Curriculum and Qualifications Reform: Final Report of the Working Group on 14–19 Reform* London: HMSO.

Department for Education and Skills (DfES) (2007) *Assessment for Learning 8 Schools Project Report,* London: DfES.*Group on Assessment.* London: DCSF.

Dewey, J. (1899) *The School and Society, Being Three Lectures by John Dewey,* Chicago: University of Chicago Press.

Dewey, J. (1934, 2005) *Art as Experience,* New York: Perigree.

Dewey, J. (1938, 1966) *Experience and Education,* London: Collier Books.

Dickens, C. (1854, 1980) *Hard Times,* Middlesex: Penguin Books.

Drummond, M-J. (1993, 2003) *Assessing Children's Learning,* London: David Fulton.

Dweck, C. S. (2000) *Self-Theories: Their Role in Motivation, Personality and Development,* Philadelphia, PA: Psychology Press.

Eisner, E. (1991) *The Enlightened Eye: Qualitative Enquiry and the Enhancement of Educational Practice,* New York: Macmillan.

Eisner, E. (2002) *The Arts and the Creation of Mind,* New Haven: Yale University Press.

Eisner, E. (2005) *Reimagining Schools: The Selected Works of Elliot W. Eisner,* London: Routledge.

Enfield, W. (1796) 'The Enquirer on Verse and Poetry'. *Monthly Magazine* 2 (6), 453–6.

Evidence for Policy and Practice Information Centre (EPPI) (2005) *A Systematic Review of the Evidence of the Reliability and Validity of Assessment by Teachers for Summative Purposes.* London Institute of Education.

Ferguson, M. (13.6.1997) Letter. *Times Educational Supplement.*

Freedman, S. W. (1991) 'Evaluating Writing Linking Large Scale Testing and Classroom Assessment'. *Centre for the Study of Writing, University of California Berkeley Occasional Paper 27,* Washington: Office of Educational Research and Improvement.

Fullan, M. (2001) *The Meaning of Educational Change,* 3rd edition. London: Routledge-Falmer.

Gibbons, S.(2009) 'Back to the future: A case study'. *English in Education* 43 (1), 19–31.

Gibbons, S. (2010) 'Revisions to the New GCSE'. *English, Drama and Media Magazine,* 16, 7–9.

Gibbons, S. (submitted) 'New Sample Tests for English'. *English, Drama and Media Magazine.*

Gibbons, S. and Marshall, B. (submitted) 'Assessing English: A trial collaborative marking project'. *English Teaching: Practice and Critique.*

Glaser, B. G. and Strauss, A. L. (1967) *The Discovery of Grounded Theory: Strategies for Qualitative Research,* Chicago: Aldine.

Great Britain Parliament House of Commons Children, Schools and Families Committee. (2008) *Testing and Assessment: Government and Ofsted Responses to the Committee's Third Report of Session 2007–2008, Fifth Special Report of Session 2007–2008. House of Commons papers 1003 2007–2008,* London: HMSO.

Hall, C. (2000) 'Reliability, Validity and Manageability'. *NZ Education Review,* **13.**

Hall, C. (2003) education.waikato.ac.nz/contracts/certstudies/English/Research/EvaluatorReport03% 20.pdf.

Hallam, S., Kirton, A., Peffers, J., Robertson, P. and Stobart, G. (2004) *Evaluation of Project 1 of the Assessment is for Learning Development Programme: Support for Professional Practice in Formative Assessment.* Edinburgh, UK: Scottish Executive.

Handy, C. (1995) *The Empty Raincoat: Making Sense of the Future,* London: Arrow Books.

Hargreaves, D. (2004) *Personalising Learning: Next Steps in Working Laterally* London: Specialist Schools Trust.

Harlen, W. (2004). 'A systematic review of the evidence of reliability and validity of assessment by teachers used for summative purposes'. In *Research Evidence in Education Library.* London: EPPI-Centre, Social Science Research Unit, Institute of Education.

Harlen, W. (2005) 'Teachers' summative practices and assessment for learning – tensions and synergies'. *The Curriculum Journal,* **16** (2), 207–23.

Hayward, L. (2007) 'Curriculum, pedagogies and assessment in Scotland: The quest for social justice. "Ah kent yir faither"'. *Assessment in Education* **14** (2), 251–68.

Hewitt, E. A. and Gordon, D. I. (1965) *English Language: An Experiment in School Assessing (first interim report),* Manchester: Joint Matriculation Board.

Hodgen, J. and Marshall, B. (2005) 'Subject Differences in formative Assessment in English and Maths'. *The Curriculum Journal* **16** (2), 153–76.

Holmes, E. (1911) *What Is and What Might Be,* London: Constable and Co. Ltd.

Hutchinson, C. and Hayward, L. (2005) 'The journey so far: Assessment for learning in Scotland'. *The Curriculum Journal,* **16** (2), 225–48.

Institute of Educational Sciences (IES) (2007a) The Nation's Report Card Reading 2007: Trial Urban Assessment Results at Grades 4 and 8.

Institute of Educational Sciences (IES) (2007b) The Nation's Report Card Reading 2007: National Assessment of Educational Progress at Grades 4 and 8.

Irwin, M. (2000) 'Results Cannot be Trusted'. *NZ Education Review,* (1 September 2000), 7.

James, M. (2004) 'Assessment of Learning, Assessment for Learning and Personalised Learning'. *Paper Presented at Goldman Sachs UK/US Conference on Urban Education.* London, December.

James, M. (2009) 'Assessment Teaching and Theories of Learning'. In J. Gardener, *Assessment and Learning.* London: Sage.

James, M. and Pedder, D. (2005) 'Professional learning as a condition for assessment for learning'. In J. Gardner (ed.) *Assessment and Learning.* London: Sage.

James, M. and Pedder, D. (2006) 'Beyond method: Assessment and learning practices and values'. *The Curriculum Journal* **17** (2), 109–38.

James, M., Black, P., Carmichael, P., Drummond, M-J., Fox, A., Honour, L., MacBeath, J., Marshall, B., McCormick, R., Pedder, D., Procter, R., Swaffield, S., Swann, J. and Wiliam, D. (2007) *Improving Learning How to Learn in Classrooms, Schools and Networks* (TLRP Improving Learning Series), London: Routledge.

Kennedy, M. (1999) 'The role of pre-service teacher education'. In L. Darling-Hammond and G. Sykes (eds) *Teaching as the Learning Profession: Handbook of Teaching and Policy,* San Francisco: Jossey Bass.

Koretz, D. (1998) 'Large-scale Portfolio Assessments in the US: evidence pertaining to the quality of measurement'. *Assessment in Education: Principles, Policy & Practice,* **5** (3), 309–34.

Koretz, D., Stecher, B. M., Klein, S. and McCaffrey, D. (1994) 'The Vermont portfolio assessment program: findings and implications'. *Educational Measurement: Issues and Practices,* **13** (3), 5–16. In B. Stecher (1998) 'The local benefits and burdens of large-scale portfolio assessment'. *Assessment in Education: Principle, Policy and Practice* **3** (5), 335–51.

LATE, (1952) 'Report of meeting on GCE Examinations in English'. In S. Gibbons, (2009) 'Back to the future: A case study'. *English in Education* **43** (1), 19–31.

LATE, (1993) *KS3: Voices from the classroom,* London: LATE.

LATE, (1995) *The Real Cost of Sats: A Report from the London Association for the Teaching of English,* London: LATE.

Leahy, T, in M. Leroux and J.O'Leary (14 October 2009) 'Tesco boss criticizes education system'. *The Times.*

Le Mahieu, P. G., Gitomerl, D. H. and Eresh, J. T. (1994) *Portfolios Beyond the Classroom: Data Quality and Qualities,* Princeton: Educational Testing Service. In B. Stecher, (1998) 'The local benefits and burdens of large-scale portfolio assessment'. *Assessment in Education: Principle, Policy and Practice* **3** (5), 335–331.

Le Mahieu, P. G., Gitomer, D. H. and Eresh, J. T. (1995) 'Portfolios in large-scale assessment: Difficult but not impossible'. *Educational Measurement: issues and practice,* **14** (3), 11–16, 25–8. In D. Koretz, (1998) 'Large-scale portfolio assessments in the US: Evidence pertaining to the quality of measurement'. *Assessment in Education: Principles, Policy & Practice,* **5** (3), 309–34.

Lipsett, A. (15 August 2008) 'US firm loses contract after SATs exam fiasco'. *The Guardian.*

Lloyd, M. (1994) 'Save English coursework: Coursework in GCSE English'. Unpublished pamphlet widely circulated through NATE to schools.

Lloyd, M. (1997) 'Dark before Dawn on Coursework?' *NATE News.*

Locke, T. (2000) 'English in the New Zealand Curriculum: Benchmarks and milestones'. *English in Australia* 127–8, 60–70.

Locke, T. (2001a) 'Curriculum assessment and the erosion of professionalism'. *New Zealand Journal of Educational Studies* **36** (1), 5–23.

Locke, T. (2001b) 'English and the NCEA: The impact of an assessment regime on curriculum practice'. *Waikato Journal of Education,* **7**, 99–116.

Locke, T. (2007) *Resisting Qualifications Reforms in New Zealand: The English Study Design as Constructive Dissent*. Rotterdam: Sense Publishers.

MacCabe, C. (1990) 'Language, Literature, Identity: Reflections on the Cox Report'. *Critical Quarterly*, **32** (4), 7–33.

Manchester Guardian, (10 October 1952) 'English Teaching in Schools'. *Guardian.*

Marshall, B. (2000) *English Teachers – The Unofficial Guide: Researching the Philosophies of English Teachers*, London: Routledge Falmer.

Marshall, B. (2001) 'Marking the Essay: Teachers subject philosophies as related to their assessment'. *English in Education*, **35** (3), 42–57.

Marshall, B. (2004a) 'Horizons not Goals: formative assessment in English teaching'. *The Curriculum Journal*, **15** (3), 101–13.

Marshall, B. (2004b) 'The write kind of knowledge: formative assessment in English teaching'. *English Teaching: Practice and Critique*, **3** (2), Web-based journal.

Masters, G. N. & McBryde, B. (1994) An Investigation of the Comparability of Teachers' Assessments of Student Folios, Tertiary Entrance Procedures Authority, Brisbane.

Maxwell, G. S. (2004) 'Progressive assessment for learning and certification: Some lessons from school-based assessment in Queensland'. Paper presented at the third conference of the Association of Commonwealth Examination and Assessment Boards redefining the roles of educational assessment. Nadi, Fiji.

Medway, P. (2003a) 'English Method'. *English and Media Magazine* **47**, 4–7.

Medway, P. (2003b) 'English as Ideas'. *Teaching Thinking* (Autumn) 20–3.

Mellon, (1975) 'National Assessment and the Teaching of Writing: Results of the first National Assessment of Educational Progess in writing. Urbana Il. National Council of Teachers'. In S.W. Freedman, (1991) *Evaluating Writing Linking Large Scale Testing and Classroom Assessment*. Centre for the study of Writing, University of California Berkeley Occasional Paper 27, Washington, Office of Educational Research and Improvement.

Miliband, D. (2003) *Personalised Learning: A Route to Excellence and Equity*, London: Specialist Schools Trust.

The National Assembly For Wales (2001) 'The Learning Country: A Paving Document A Comprehensive Education and Lifelong Learning Programme to 2010 in Wales'. http://wales.gov.uk/docs/dcells/publications/091023learningcountryen.pdf.

National Curriculum Board (2009) 'Shape of the Curriculum: English. Canberra, Commonwealth of Australia'. http://www.acara.edu.au/verve/_resources/Australian_Curriculum_-_English.pdf.

National Oracy Project (1991) *Teaching Talking and Learning at Key Stage 3*, London: NCC/NOP.

The National Strategies (2008) *Assessing Pupils' Progress in English at Key Stage 3: Assessment Guidelines*, London: DCSF.

National Writing Project (1989a) *Writing and Learning*, Surrey: Thomas Nelson and Sons Ltd.

National Writing Project (1989b) *Audiences for Writing*, Surrey: Thomas Nelson and Sons Ltd.

Ofsted, (2007) *Poetry in Schools: A Survey of Practice 2006/7*, London: HMSO.

Perrenoud, P. (1998) 'From formative evaluation to a controlled regulation of learning processes. Towards a wider conceptual field'. *Assessment in Education: Principles, Policy and Practice* **5** (1), 85–102.

Petch, J. A. (1967) *English Language: An Experiment in Assessing Second Interim Report*, Manchester: Joint Matriculation Board.

Pitfield, M. (2006) 'Making a crisis out of a drama: the relationship between English and Drama within the English curriculum for ages 11–14'. *Changing English* **13** (1), 97–109.

Pitman, J. A., O'Brien, J. E. and Mc Callow, J. E. 1999, 'High quality assessment: We are what we believe and do'. Paper presented at the IAEA Conference, Bled, Slovenia, May.

Protherough, R., Atkinson J. and Fawcett J. (1989) *The Effective Teaching of English*, London: Longman.

Qualifications and Curriculum Authority (Myhill, D.) (1999) *Improving Writing at Key Stage 3 and 4*, London, QCA Publications Qualifications and Curriculum Authority (2005) *English 21 Playback: A National Conversation on the Teaching of English.* London: HMSO.

Qualifications and Curriculum Authority (2005) *Taking English Forward*, London: HMSO.

Qualifications and Curriculum Authority (2006a) *Monitoring Pupils' Progress in English at Key Stage 3. Final Report of the 2003–2005 Pilot*, London: QCA.

Qualifications Curriculum Authority (2006b) *Functional Skills Draft Standards: English, Mathematics and ICT,* London: HMSO.

Qualifications and Curriculum Authority, (2009a) *Assessing Pupils' Progress: Assessment at the Heart of Learning*, London: HMSO.

Qualifications and Curriculum Authority (2009b) *Delivering Functional Skills: Lessons Learnt from the Pilot*, London: HMSO.

Queensland (2009a) Retrieved 7 January 2010 from http://www.qsa.qld.edu.au/assessment/586.html.

Queensland (2009b) Random tests. Retrieved 8 January 2010 from http://www.qsa.qld.edu.au/downloads/assessment/assess_snr_rpt_random_2009.pdf.

The Radford Report (1970) *Queensland. Committee Appointed to Review the System of Public Examinations for Queensland Secondary School Students and to Make Recommendations for the Assessment of Student's Achievements.* Brisbane: Department of Education, Queensland.

Rooke, H. M. and Hewitt, E. A. (1970) *An Experimental Scheme of School Assessment in Ordinary Level English Language: Third report*, Manchester: Joint Matriculation Board.

Royal Shakespeare Company (2008) Stand Up for Shakespeare http://www.rsc.org.uk/standupforshakespeare/content/03_SeeItLive.aspx.

Rowe, M. B. (1974) 'Wait-time and rewards as instructional variables, their influence in language, logic and fate control'. Part 1: wait time. Journal of Research in Science Teaching, **11** (3), 263–79.

Sadler, R. (1989). 'Formative assessment and the design of instructional systems'. *Instructional Science*, **18** (2), 119–44.

Sadler, R. (2006) 'Bringing students into the "guild": Making assessment work directly for learning'. Paper presented at QUT School of Early Childhood Surfair on Marcoola Beach, 9–10 November 2006.

Sadler, R. (2009) 'Transforming Holistic Assessment and Grading into a Vehicle for Complex Learning'. In G. Joughin (ed.) *Assesment, Learning and Judgement in Higher Education*, Amsterdam: Springer Netherlands.

Scott, E., Berkeley, G., Howell, M., Schuntner, L. Walker, R. and Winkle, L. [The Scott Report] (1978) *A Review of School-based Assessment in Queensland Secondary Schools.* Brisbane: Board of Secondary School Studies.

Scottish Office Education Department (1991) *Curriculum and assessment in Scotland: national guidelines: English language 5–14*, Edinburgh: HMSO.

Sfard, A. (1998) 'On two metaphors for learning and the dangers of choosing just one'. *Educational Researcher*, **27**, 4–13.

Smith, G. A. (1978) *JMB Experience of the Moderation of Internal Assessments*, Manchester: Joint Matriculation Board.

Smith, L. (2009) 'Beyond APP'. Unpublished Article.

Stecher, B. (1998) 'The local benefits and burdens of large-scale portfolio assessment'. *Assessment in Education: Principle, Policy and Practice* **3** (5), 335–331.

Thomas, W. H., Storms, B. A., Sheingold, K., Heller, J. J., Paulukonis, S. T., Nunez, A. M. and Wing, J. Y. (1995) *California Learning Assessment System: Portfolio Assessment Research and Development Project. Final Report* (Princeton, Educational Testing Service, Center for Performance Assessment). In B. Stecher, (1998) 'The local benefits and burdens of large-scale portfolio assessment'. *Assessment in Education: Principle, Policy and Practice* **3** (5), 335–331.

Torrance, H. and Pryor, J. (1998) *Investigating Formative Assessment: Teaching, Learning and Assessment in the Classroom*, Buckingham: Open University Press.

Vygotsky, L. S. (1978) *Thought and Language*, Cambridge, MA: Harvard University Press.

Wiliam, D. (1994) 'Assessing authentic tasks: Alternatives to mark–schemes'. *Nordic Studies in Mathematics Education*, **2** (1), 48–68.

Wiliam, D. (1996) 'Standards in Education: A matter of trust'. *The Curriculum Journal*, **7** (3), 293–306.

Wiliam, D. (1998) 'The Validity of Teachers' Assessments'. Paper presented at the 22nd annual conference of the International Group for the Psychology of Mathematics Education, Stellenbosch, South Africa.

Wiliam, D. (2009) 'Assessment for Learning: Why no profile in US policy'. In In J. Gardener (ed.), *Assessment and Learning*, London: Sage.

Williams, R. (1961) *The Long Revolution*, London: Penguin.

Wilson, (1965) Forward. In E. A. Hewitt and D. I. Gordon (eds) *English Language: An Experiment in School Assessing (first interim report)*, Manchester: Joint Matriculation Board.

WJEC/CBAC (2008) *Key Stage 3 Teacher Assessment Core Subject External Moderation 2009: Guidance for selection of sample evidence for resubmission for external moderation*, Pontyprydd, WJEC.

Wollstonecraft, M. (1789, 15 January 2003) web address http.duke.usask.ca/~vargo/barbould/related_texts/wollstonecraft.html.

Index